Accidents Happen

Seven Short Plays by
J. Michael DeAngelis,
Pete Barry, and
John P. Dowgin

A SAMUEL FRENCH ACTING EDITION

SAMUEL FRENCH

FOUNDED 1830

NEW YORK HOLLYWOOD LONDON TORONTO

SAMUELFRENCH.COM

ISBN 978-0-573-69864-4   Printed in U.S.A.   #29679

MUSIC USE NOTE

IMPORTANT BILLING AND CREDIT
REQUIREMENTS

The Clive Way was originally presented by The Porch Room as part of *Five Cornered Thinking* at The New York Comedy Club on September 8-16, 2000. The cast was as follows:

LIONEL . . . . Pete Barry

MICKEY . . . . Adam B. Kaufman

HAROLD . . . . Brian Sherman

DOCTOR POOTRAM . . . . .Eric Werner

CLIVE GARRISON . . . . .John P. Dowgin

Hangman was originally presented by The Porch Room as part of *Five Cornered Thinking* at the New York Comedy Club on September 8-16, 2000. The cast was as follows:

DRENTH . . . . Adam B. Kaufman

YANKUS . . . . .John P. Dowgin

TETWILLIGER . . . . Brian Sherman

HARMON . . . . .Eric Werner

JONES . . . . Pete Barry

The Banderscott was originally produced by The Porch Room in *Burt Reynolds' Amazing Napalm Powered Oven (And Other Paid Programming)* in the 2001 New York Fringe Festival. The cast was as follows:

BOB HENDERSON . . . . Adam B. Kaufman

EILEEN . . . . Ruben Ortiz

HARCOURT McALLISTER . . . . Pete Barry

DR. THINN . . . . Ruben Ortiz

TERRY . . . . Faith Agnew Dowgin

TONY . . . . Tony Grinage

GALLAGHER . . . . Skip Moore

BURT REYNOLDS . . . . Zachary R. Mannheimer

Nine Point Eight Meters Per Second Per Second was a finalist in the 34th Samuel French Off-Off Broadway Festival. It was performed on July 18th & 19th, 2009. The production was directed by J. Michael DeAngelis. The cast was as follows:

BALTHAZAR KENT . . . . Pete Barry

ACCIDENTS HAPPEN was first produced in full at The Circle Players in Piscataway, New Jersey on July 11, 2008. The performances were directed by the authors, with sound design by Pete Barry, technical assistance by Gordon Wiener. The production stage manager was Tina Lee, with additional material by Serena Halley. The cast was as follows:

ACCIDENTS HAPPEN by J. Michael DeAngelis

AIRLINE HOSTESS	Elizabeth Tozour Lafargue
STEWARDESS	Lauren Plummer

NINE POINT EIGHT METERS PER SECOND PER SECOND, by Pete Barry

BALTHAZAR KENT	John P. Dowgin

REUNION SPECIAL, by J. Michael DeAngelis

DUNCAN GORCYNZSKI	Ivan Rushfield
CYRUS O'LEARY	Jon Heron
MAGGIE O'LEARY	Cathy Zouves-Wroebel
EDDIE TAYLOR	Danny Siegel
NANCY NOBLE	Lauren Plummer
JILLIAN McMILLAN	Elizabeth Tozour Lafargue

THE CLIVE WAY, by John P. Dowgin

LIONEL	Ed Faver
MICKEY	Matt Lafargue
HAROLD	David C. Neal
DOCTOR POOTRAM	Jon Heron
CLIVE GARRISON	Shaka Malik
MONOTONE VOICE	Bernice Woldman

HANGMAN, by Pete Barry

DRENTH	Serena Halley
YANKUS	Pete Barry
TETWILLIGER	Matt Lafargue
JONES	Shaka Malik
HARMON	Andrew Young

TRICKS OF THE TRADE, by John P. Dowgin

EDDIE	David C. Neal
RALPH	Randall McCann
KEN	Ed Faver

THE BANDERSCOTT, by Pete Barry

BOB HENDERSON	John P. Dowgin
EILEEN	Matt Lafargue
HARCOURT McALLISTER	J. Michael DeAngelis
DR. THINN	Pete Barry
TERRY	Serena Halley
TONY	Randall McCann
RON POPIEL	Matt Lafargue
SHERMAN THE OCTOPUS	Himself

ACCIDENTS HAPPEN was nominated for five NJACT Perry Awards: Outstanding Production of an Original Play*; Outstanding Supporting Actor – Jon Heron*; Outstanding Supporting Actor – Shaka Malik; Outstanding Supporting Actress – Cathy Zouves-Wroebel; Outstanding Stage Management of a Play – Tina Lee*

*Winner.

AUTHORS' NOTE

The plays in this collection may be performed as an entire evening's entertainment or as standalone one acts. When performed as an entire collection, an intermission should be inserted after *THE CLIVE WAY*.

CONTENTS

I.

ACCIDENTS HAPPEN

by J. Michael DeAngelis

THE CHARACTERS

AIRLINE HOST or **HOSTESS**
STEWARDESS or **STEWARD**

THE SETTING

Your theater. Tonight.

*(Enter **AIRLINE HOST** and a **STEWARDESS** [or any combination of sexes thereof].)*

*(The **HOST** speaks, while the **STEWARDESS** performs all the standard safety gestures like a crazed smiling robot.)*

HOST. Good evening and thank you for flying [name of theater company]. Our captain tonight is [director or producer], who will be taking us to a cruising altitude of approximately three feet. Your flight tonight will last approximately two hours, with one fifteen-minute intermission. We ask that you turn off all electronic devices, including cell phones and pagers. If you have a pager, 1988 called and wants it back.

*(The **STEWARDESS** makes the sign for "loser" by making an L shape with her fingers and holding it over her head.)*

Please refrain from taking flash photography, as our lawyers spend enough time removing pictures of us from the internet as it is.

*(**STEWARDESS** covers herself as if nude.)*

In the case of an emergency, exits are located here, here and here – and in the event of a fire or other disaster, please stampede quickly and violently out of the theater in order to save yourselves. If you are traveling with small children, they make excellent flotation devices in the event of a water landing. As part of cost saving measures, there are no oxygen masks available on this flight. In case of an emergency, phones are located in the seat in front of you so that you may make your final farewells to loved ones. All calls cost a minimum of $100 and may be paid by Visa or Mastercard.

*(The **STEWARDESS** demonstrates swiping a credit card.)*

HOST. *(cont.)* Don't worry, though. The chances of something going wrong are extremely slim.

(A tremendous boom is heard offstage.)

Then again…accidents happen.

(blackout)

(The sound of a commercial airliner lifting off, segueing directly into "Nine Point Eight Meters Per Second Per Second" *when performed together.)*

II.

NINE POINT EIGHT METERS PER SECOND PER SECOND

by Pete Barry

CHARACTERS

BALTHAZAR KENT

(A single, comfortable chair in the void; slight movement and a sound of wind make it clear that the chair is plummeting through the atmosphere.)

*(**BALTHAZAR KENT**, a wiry haired English gentleman, dozes.)*

(He jolts awake, looks around, and digs his Blackberry out of his pocket.)

(He dials.)

BALTHAZAR. Hullo?

Yes. I'd like to speak to a manager.

Well you see I was hopping your flight five-four-nine from Heathrow to Los Angeles, and now I appear to be falling out of the sky.

Yes, I'll hold.

(Pushes a button on the Blackberry.)

Michael. I'll be late to the four o'clock in California. Stall the meeting. Call me back. Quickly.

(Pushes another button.)

Hullo? Yes, sir, I'm falling. Still in my seat, though. It seems to have come with me.

Where am I? Somewhere between London and Los Angeles. I know we had reached North America. I'm sorry if I can't be more specific.

I'd like to resolve this problem within the next two minutes, if possible.

I'm assuming that's the maximum amount of time I have before I hit the ground.

Yes, sir, I did the differential calculus, taking into account my drag, vector velocity, and the earth's gravitational pull at nine point eight meters per second per second.

How do I know the earth's gravity? The wonders of a liberal education.

Yes, I'm sure you are unfamiliar with liberal education, sir. Otherwise you would not be answering the telephone in an airport terminal.

Hold please.

(pushes a button)

Michael.

Get that bloke from accounting, the corpulent fellow, Hinkley. Ask him if it's true that if one's parachute should fail to open during freefall one should pump one's legs as if running as ground approaches. I've heard that somewhere. And call my wife and tell her to up my life insurance policy, if she knows what's good for her. Call me back. No buts, Michael.

(pushes a button)

Yes, sir, where were we? It would help if you could tell me how to unfasten this belt buckle.

The chair is a floatation device? I hardly believe that helps if I hit the ground at several hundred miles per hour.

I highly doubt that it will bounce.

Where is the plane? Sir, it's your company's plane. It wasn't my responsibility to keep abreast of it.

It may have been destroyed in a terrorist attack, or perhaps my seat was inadvertently sucked out of a fire exit.

Frankly, sir, if the engineers who constructed that aeroplane are of your caliber of intelligence, it is quite possible that the entire machine spontaneously burst into its component sheet metal.

I just don't see how this is my problem.

Please hold.

(pushes a button)

Simone, darling, how are you? Quickly, darling, up my accidental death policy.

No I don't believe it's going to matter, I'm going to pump my legs as I hit the ground, once I get out of this chair. Still, it's best to be prepared.

Well, I'm not sure if there's anything wrong with the plane. I'm not on the plane. Why is everyone so concerned about the damn plane?

Yes, I'm plummeting to earth, darling.

How is this my fault?

You tell me not to go to the office every day of the week! Your horoscope has been wrong several hundred thousand times to date!

Am I wearing my good suit?

HEAVEN FORBID I SHOULD FALL OUT OF AN AIRPLANE AND IT NOT BE TO YOUR EXACT SPECIFICATIONS, MADAM!

Look, got to resolve this thing, I'll call you back.

(pushes a button)

Yes, have you figured out this seat belt yet?

Michael?

Have you got Hinkley?

Have you stalled the meeting?

Then what are you calling me for?

I called you? Don't be stupid, Michael, do what I'm asking you to.

(pushes a button)

Hello, who is this, now?

Yes, the seat buckle is stuck.

Lovely.

Cut it? Sir, your company would have relieved me of my undergarments if they believed I could have used them as a sharp weapon.

Look, perhaps you have some sort of owner's manual.

I can't see how I can start running while sitting down.

All right, I'll try it.

(He fiddles with the buckle, and it pops open.)

Oh, look at that, something you suggested actually worked.

Fine, I'm abandoning the chair.

(He slides out of the chair, looks down, and scuttles back into it.)

SHIT.

Shit. All right. It's not land. It's water. The ocean. Shit. I wasn't prepared for this. I suppose we hadn't reached the continent. All right. I'm back in the chair. Wait. Is hitting water like hitting the ground? Maybe I could still pump my legs. Or will I sink right through? Should I buckle in? Or not buckle in? All right. Is this chair solid? Is that good or bad? Should I hold my breath? Will the impact harm me if I do? Are you there? Is this chair safe? Oh my God is that a shark? Is it true that –

(Black, and SPLASH, and the deep quiet sound of immersion in water.)

(Then the gentle white noise of ocean waves.)

(Lights up.)

(Balthazar lies motionless in the chair, mouth wide open.)

(His Blackberry beeps.)

(Beeps.)

(Beeps.)

(He sits up and answers it.)

Hullo, yes?

(long pause)

Is Portia here?

Well let me check.

No, sorry, I don't believe Portia is here right now, you see I'm in the middle of the FUCKING OCEAN.

Yes I believe you have a wrong number. Now –

NO NO WAIT DON'T HANG UP.

Are you an American?

A Canadian? Even better.

You must alert the authorities. The, Mounties, or whatever you have.

My name is Balthazar Kent, and I am an extremely important –

What?

Yes, Balthazar, yes that really is my name.

Well, ha ha ha, and what's your name?

Well, hello, Marta, you sound like a very stupid girl.

Oh, you're top of your class at university? And employee of the week?

Well let me ask you this, Marta, did you clear over one point six million pounds for your company last quarter?

Oh, you didn't?

Well, you see, I did, Marta. So I'm rather an important fellow. And I'm currently late for a meeting in California. So if you've any brains in your head at all, you'll call the authorities right now, so they can get me to my meeting.

NO DON'T HANG UP.

Please ask a manager or someone else to make the call for you.

Thank you.

What is this, anyway? A telemarketing firm?

Why on earth are you calling a British mobile number?

Your manager has the authorities? Can you patch me through or whatever?

Hullo? Is this the Mounties?

Oh, you're just the regular police, then.

I can barely hear you, sir.

Well I am in the middle of the ocean.

The Atlantic, I presume.

I was on an intercontinental flight to Los Angeles, and –

Oh, on the news, eh?

Do you know what happened?

(long pause)

You have got to be kidding me.

(pause)

I am never, ever, ever, ever, flying with this company again.

No, I suggest you don't, either.

What do you mean?

Just come pick me up.

I don't know, don't you people have helicopters?

I'm on a bloody Blackberry! Can't it be tracked with some kind of satellite triangulation?

Well, why don't you ask Marta? She's top of her class at university!

NO DON'T –

Yes, hello Marta, I was just wondering if you were studying satellite transmissions or global positioning systems at university.

You're studying theater. How nice.

Yes, you're right we did have two. Shakespeare and Milton. We didn't produce a single other author or poet.

Well of course I'm glad to be talking to you, Marta, I was getting worried I wouldn't hear the dulcet tones of your voice again.

No I won't explain what "dulcet" means. You should have studied that at university.

Look, I'm just getting a little tired of people not doing what I'm asking them to.

What time is it in California? I can't keep these clients waiting forever.

Yes, Marta, I really am in the middle of the ocean.

Will I die? What kind of bloody morbid question is that? How could I possibly calculate that kind of probability?

Am I prepared to die? What on earth do you…?

HAHAHAHAHAHAHAHAHA!

I'm sorry, Marta, the signal is very bad. I must not have heard you properly. I swear I thought you asked me…

(pause)

…if Jesus Christ was my Lord and Savior.

You did just ask me that, didn't you?

Is he?

Erm.

(pause)

Yes. Yes he is, Marta.

It is good news, isn't it?

We wouldn't want to have to have a christening at a time like this.

I suppose there is plenty of water around for it and all, but still.

Listen, Marta, getting back to this I'm-stuck-in-the-middle-of-the-Atlantic bit.

You see, I must get to this meeting. Are you connected to the internet?

Fantastic. Would you navigate to a web address for me? Certainly.

W-w-w dot l-e-m-p-s-h-i-r-e, dot co. Oh, dot u-k.

No, no, not "o-u-k." Just, Lempshire, dot co, dot u-k.

Yes, "uck."

Well, that's the web address.

What is "uck"?

That would be "yoo-kay."

For "United Kingdom."

What is the United Kingdom?

It's bloody England, you stupid bird!

What is it United with? Scotland and Wales, I suppose. A bit of Ireland.

You yourself, in fact, used to be united with the British Empire.

Well, not you specifically. Your country.

Unless – you're not in Quebec, are you?

Then yes, you were a part of the Empire. In fact, Quebec, too, now that I think about it. We got that from the French, tall lot of good Quebec ever did us.

What do you mean, you don't believe me? You don't know this? You're in university, for God's sakes!

Yes, Marta, I apologize for taking the Lord's name in vain.

Have you got the site yet?

Fantastic.

Click on "Management."

Look for "Balthazar Kent."

Oh, God, don't they even teach spelling in Canada? Kent starts with a "K."

I'm starting to wish I had gotten some bloody American.

Good, scroll down.

Executive-level Vice Presidents.

There I am! Fantastic. What does it say?

(long pause)

You're joking.

They must have pronounced me dead before the authorities did.

What?

Replaced?

Carolyn Williams?

That fat bitch!

I'm not in the cold ground three hours, and she's already got my bloody job!

Oh my God the meeting.

She's probably there.

Go to login!

Login, woman, for the life of you!

Username k-e-n-t-b password x-t-three-capital-k-four-eight!

Enter!

Click "Meeting Schedule"!

Does it say rescheduled?

No?

Meeting lead Carolyn Williams?

NO!

Take dictation, Marta!

In the post reply box!

This is VP Kent! Am not dead! Am in fact alive! Meeting to NOT proceed. Request postponement until further notice! Enter!

What?

What do you mean closed?

Wait!

Look at the bottom right!

Does it say CLOSED?

NOOOOOOOOOOOOOOOOOO!

(Silence. **BALTHAZAR** *leans back.)*

Yes, Marta, I'm still here. Shut it down.

Yes it's bad.

It means that the meeting was held without me.

It means that I will not meet the client, and Carolyn already has.

Which in turn means that I'm likely already out of a job.

It's over.

(silence)

My life no longer has any purpose. I am floating in the middle of the ocean. I no longer need to meet my appointment. My entire schedule is meaningless. I am as if one dead.

You may as well leave me out here. I have nowhere to be.

What possible bright side, Marta?

No, I don't have any family.

Well, my wife.

And son.

They hate me.

Why? I suppose because I hate them.

Well you don't notice how sad it is, actually, when you have a sufficient number of meetings.

Meetings are what hold modern society together, from playdates to funeral arrangements. Human beings are simply aggregates of quantum particles colliding at random. Meetings provide structure to the human experience. Without meetings, we are in chaos.

I feel so empty.

I could just float here. In the ocean. Watch the sharks and the jellyfish.

I could live here, possibly. Like a hermit. Fashion a harpoon from my seatbelt. Eat raw fish. Harvest rain and dew for drinking water. Day becomes night. The sting of the cold air will become familiar. This will be all I know.

But for now, Marta, I'll just talk to you, if you don't mind, until my battery dies. You will be the last human being I ever speak to.

And then I will be alone. In the middle of the ocean. A monk adrift in the endless surf.

(silence)

What do you mean, I'm not in the middle of the ocean?

Lake Superior?

How the hell do you know that?

They've triangulated my position?

So I'm saved?

I'm saved!

How big is Lake Superior?

(pause)

Well, that's not much better, now, is it?

Yes, I understand why it's called "Superior."

What is the matter with you, Marta?

I'd just come to terms with my situation, and you raise my spirits only to dash them again on the broken steps of Fate!

Well, what would Jesus do, Marta?

You know what I think he'd do? He'd –

(HOOOOOONK. An earsplitting horn.)

It's a ship. It's a ship, Marta! It's coming right for me! Hey! HEY! Ah. Turn! Turn port, or starboard, or whatever the hell way you turn, just turn! You're coming right at me! Hey! HEY –

(black)

(Balthazar's screams are drowned in a deafening rush of water.)

(The sound of clanking chains.)

(Lights up.)

(The chair is askew, perhaps upside down. **BALTHAZAR** *sits on top, still on his Blackberry.)*

Yes, Michael, I'm aware that –

(The chair rocks.)

Excuse me.

(He looks up.)

Could you wonderful gentlemen be a bit more careful? You're very right. I don't know how a crane works. Never mind! I'll try to relax!

(He returns to his phone conversation.)

Sorry, Michael, where was I?

Thank you.

So everyone can hear me right now? The connection isn't spotty?

That's fine. I just want them to know that what I have to say is very important. Perhaps the most important thing I've ever said.

Tell me when.

(pause)

Hello, ladies and gentlemen. Please excuse the connection, I am in fact thirteen miles off shore.

Thank you. Yes, thank you, Carolyn.

And I'm glad that you were ready to step in, Carolyn. When I hit the water I thought I was dead. In a way I was. Powerless, cold, cut off, alone. At the mercy of God's universe. And when I found out I'd been given up for dead, well. That was a hard hit.

I began to realize that the only real difference between my life in the ocean and my life at home was the speed and number of events. In neither place did I feel anything but indignant rage. In neither place did I have any control over the course of my life. In neither place did I have any meaningful human relationship, with you, my coworkers, or with my wife and son. Might I not be better off floating in the ocean than visiting pain upon my friends and family, for all my absence, my austerity, my blind drive to serve only myself?

(He coughs.)

Excuse me. I believe I may be having some hypothermia, I'll try to be more brief. I'm not entirely sure if my right leg can be saved.

So I asked you here today, ladies and gentlemen, not to ask for reinstatement, but to confer on you the truth of my spiritual journey. Carolyn, I know you have family. Have you seen them lately? Daniel, you have brothers. Call them and tell them you love them. Do not float in your own icy ocean waters. Life is not about meetings. Life is about the people in the meetings.

Thank you.

Yes Carolyn?

Oh, I don't know, what with everything that's happened –

Well I'll think about it. If I'm needed, then certainly

I'll step back into the role. I'll call the client tomorrow and explain.

Yes, thank you, Carolyn. Please don't cry, my dear.

I know. Why don't you sign off and call them right now?

Certainly, dear.

(pause)

Is she gone? Thank God.

SHE TOOK MY FUCKING JOB?

And none of you questioned that?

Yes, I'd say you'd better not if you don't want a lawsuit in the future. "Dead man wants job back" – that'll be in all the tabloids.

Hopefully she's writing her resignation in tears right now.

Well then. What lesson have we learned here?

That's right, Michael! Don't rush into things.

Good.

What time is it in London, now?

Nine o'clock Saturday morning. Fine. Let's meet this afternoon, two o'clock, conference call.

You've what, Ronald?

Oh, you'll have to cancel cricket practice? How terrible I've got a GANGRENOUS LEG. Tell your cricket pals to shove it.

See you all at two o'clock, sharp.

Michael!

Repopulate my schedule, please. It must have been erased somehow.

Let me check.

(He toggles through the Blackberry's menus. He smiles.)

Ahhh.

Thank you Michael.

Enjoy your weekend. Keep your phone on! I'll see you Monday. Bright and early.

(He hangs up and pockets the Blackberry. Clang from the chain.)

Watch it, you hives of sexually transmitted disease! Slowly!

(black)

III.

REUNION SPECIAL

by J. Michael DeAngelis

CHARACTERS

DUNCAN GORCZYNSKI – A former child star, now in hard times. 30s.

CYRUS O'LEARY – Fawning owner of the funeral parlor. Mid to late
50s.

MAGGIE O'LEARY – Cyrus's excitable sister. Slightly dumpy. Late 40s.

EDDIE TAYLOR – Former child star, now a handsome movie star. 30s.

NANCY NOBLE – Former child star, sexual, domineering and cold. 30s.

JILLIAN MCMILLAN – Former child star, soft spoken, warm and flowery. 30s.

TIME

The Present

PLACE

O'Leary's Funeral Boutique, outside Hollywood, California

(Lights up on a small room in the back of a funeral home. It is sparse with several chairs randomly placed around and a long table upstage center. The table contains a coffee urn and various finger foods. Also on the table is a framed headshot of Dirk Howard, former television star.)

*(At rise, **DUNCAN GORCZYNSKI** is sitting at a chair by the table. He is in his thirties, dressed in black slacks with a matching black blazer, but his otherwise somber look is thrown by a tasteless Hawaiian shirt and a generally unkempt feel about him. He sits, nervously fidgeting and occasionally popping little sandwiches from the table into his mouth. He keeps checking his watch.)*

*(Someone approaches and **DUNCAN** excitedly gets up. **CYRUS O'LEARY**, the somewhat tacky looking owner of the funeral home, enters. **DUNCAN**'s disappointment can not be hidden – he was expecting someone else. **CYRUS** is cheery and eager to please.)*

CYRUS. Can I get you anything, Mr. Gorczynski? Is the coffee done brewing?

DUNCAN. Is anybody else here yet?

CYRUS. No, not yet. Danish?

DUNCAN. No, thanks.

CYRUS. Fresh made this morning. Little old Pakistani lady down the street makes them. Best in town. I didn't even know they HAD danish in Pakistan. Usually, when I do these sort of catered affairs, I just go to the wholesale club, but given this occasion, I thought I'd spring –

DUNCAN. Mr. O'Leary, maybe you should go back out to the viewing room. Someone might walk in and think they missed the whole thing.

31

CYRUS. It's fine, it's fine. My sister-slash-assistant is out there. She'll show any of your guests back here if they arrive.

DUNCAN. *When* they arrive.

CYRUS. Of course. Meanwhile, please, make yourself comfortable.

(DUNCAN sits back down. CYRUS pours himself a cup of coffee and sits opposite DUNCAN. CYRUS stares across the room at him like an overjoyed child.)

DUNCAN. Mr. O'Leary, for the last time – please stop staring!

CYRUS. I'm sorry. I'm sorry! I can't help it. It's just that I'm such…

DUNCAN. Such a big fan, I know.

CYRUS. Guilty as charged!! This is such a thrill. I mean, you can't imagine how over the moon I was when you called about having this memorial service for Mr. Howard. I mean, a celebrity memorial service *here?* I bury drunk Irish cops and nursing home drop outs, not TV stars. The entire cast of *Oh, Spaz* – Saturday mornings at 11 am, 1993-1997 – together again in MY funeral home! It's like a command performance just for me.

DUNCAN. You don't get out much, do you?

CYRUS. *(still cheery)* No. *(He pops a Danish in his mouth.)* You kids must have really loved him.

DUNCAN. Who?

CYRUS. Dirk Howard, silly. The man who played your principal-slash-nemesis-slash-confidant. I guess after five years on television together, you really do become close. I mean, you went to all this trouble to have a memorial service for him when nobody else would.

DUNCAN. *(distractedly)* Yes, yes. He was like a father to me.

CYRUS. I hate to bring it up – but, it all seemed so deliciously scandalous. A faded Saturday morning TV star just up and disappears. I heard on Access Hollywood that some people think it's all just a tax scam...then again, maybe it was the old "sniff sniff" *(indicates snorting cocaine).* But listen to me, speaking ill of the dead... or the missing...or...whatever Mr. Howard is.

DUNCAN. *(agitated)* His family had him declared legally dead last week. And they didn't want a memorial service – no press, no attention, they just want to move on. But I needed to have this memorial and I needed the others to come, so I picked this place. A run down nothing of a funeral home where nobody would think to snoop around.

CYRUS. *(oblivious)* Coffee?

DUNCAN. No. No coffee. Thank you.

(With a burst of energy enters **MAGGIE O'LEARY**, **CYRUS***'s sister and assistant.)*

MAGGIE. Cyrus! Cyrus! HE'S HERE!

DUNCAN. Eddie?

MAGGIE. It must be him – a huge Corvette just pulled up the drive. The kind with the black, brushed metal look, like he drove in *The Apocalypse Twelve.*

CYRUS. I can't believe it. Oh, Maggie – this is just the living end! Quick, quick, show him in!

*(***MAGGIE** *runs off.* **DUNCAN** *tries to smooth out his clothes and make himself seem as presentable as possible.* **CYRUS** *pours a fresh cup of coffee.)*

DUNCAN. I haven't seen this guy in over a decade.

CYRUS. Well, he came. I'm sure it will be just like old times.

MAGGIE. *(offstage)* Right through here, Mr. Taylor.

*(***MAGGIE** *re-enters, escorting* **EDDIE TAYLOR**, *an amazingly good-looking movie star about the same age as Duncan. He is dressed to the nines in a black suit and tie, with black leather shoes polished like fine china. He looks around, uneasy of the surroundings.)*

DUNCAN. Eddie!

EDDIE. Look, man, no autographs, I'm here for a… Duncan?

DUNCAN. It's me!

*(An awkward pause. Then **EDDIE** smiles and gives **DUNCAN** a big hug.)*

EDDIE. It's good to see you, man! Jesus, little Duncan Gorczynski all grown up! Look at you!

DUNCAN. Look at me? Look at YOU! Mr. Golden Globe nominee!

EDDIE. Oh please, it was a terrible movie.

CYRUS. *(as he hands **EDDIE** the coffee)* Oh no! Oh no! It was wonderful! I saw it twice in one weekend! Just the title alone – *The Nocturnal Voyeur* – just to die for! Cyrus O'Leary, proprietor…and movie buff.

DUNCAN. Mr. O'Leary perhaps you could give us a moment alone…to mourn?

CYRUS. Oh, of course. Maggie and I will wait outside for your other guests.

DUNCAN. Thank you.

O'LEARY. Come along, Mags.

*(**CYRUS** and **MAGGIE** both start to exit, their eyes fixed on **EDDIE** – star struck. Just as she's offstage we overhear **MAGGIE**)*

MAGGIE. *(off)* My God, I think I wet my pants just looking at him.

*(**EDDIE** and **DUNCAN** laugh at the absurdity of their hosts.)*

EDDIE. Duncan "Spaz" Gorczynski. Dorky Gorky!

DUNCAN. Oh God. *(beat)* Look at you, Eddie. You're so "Hollywood" now! More than I could ever be!

EDDIE. So what have you been up to, man?

DUNCAN. Well, uh – not too much. I was on the stand up circuit for a while, but I think my act was just a little too "out there" for the comedy club crowd. Nothing but a bunch of drunks. Anyway, I've got my hand in a computer repair business – and of course I do the conventions and autograph sessions. But I guess you know all about that, Mr. Golden Globes!

EDDIE. They don't have Golden Globe nominee conventions, Duncan.

*(An awkward laugh. **EDDIE** sees the picture of Dirk Howard on the buffet.)*

EDDIE. Poor old, Dirk, huh? You know, I feel bad – he really was a decent guy I guess, but I never saw him as anything more than his character, you know? To me, he was just the annoying principal – but looking back I can remember him trying to give me acting tips and stuff. That was a decent thing to do, you know. Lord knows we needed it.

DUNCAN. *(doing his best at being sincere)* Sure wish we could go back and tell him thanks. To be on the set again, the whole gang. Man, if we ever got the chance, I think we'd owe it to Dirk.

EDDIE. I think we're all a bit too busy – and expensive – for the Sunday Night Movie reunion special.

DUNCAN. Well, maybe you are.

EDDIE. Oh come on, you're still doing movies aren't you? You were always doing pictures, even when we were kids – way before I was.

DUNCAN. The last movie I made went straight to DVD.

EDDIE. Hey, there's big money there. Lots of residuals.

DUNCAN. It was five years ago, Eddie. It was called *White Trash Booty Call.* Not exactly a cash cow.

EDDIE. Hey, something will happen for you. Lord knows I made plenty of shit before the good parts started coming in.

DUNCAN. Well, I think that maybe there is something on the horizon…

*(He starts to produce something from his suit pocket when the last two guests arrive – **NANCY NOBLE** and **JILLIAN MCMILLAN**. **NANCY** is dressed to kill in a tight*

black dress with a red leather jacket. **JILLIAN** *has a slightly more flowery feel about her, but still gets the guys' attention.* **JILLIAN** *is definitely beta dog to* **NANCY** *– and likes it that way.)*

(They are followed in by an adoring **MAGGIE** *and* **CYRUS**.*)*

NANCY. Eddie Taylor, why don't you take me out to the parking lot and take me round the world like we were sixteen again? I've got handcuffs in my bag.

EDDIE. *(slightly embarrassed)* Nancy Noble. How the hell are you?

NANCY. Give me fifteen minutes and you'll find out.

*(***EDDIE** *goes to give her a hug, but she just stands there – her eyes challenging him. Not knowing what to do,* **EDDIE** *merely gives her a peck on the cheek.)*

NANCY. I liked it better when we were sixteen. Jillian, speak.

JILLIAN. Hey, Eddie.

EDDIE. Hey, Jill.

*(***JILLIAN** *gives a look to* **NANCY** *who just rolls her eyes and nods – giving permission for* **JILLIAN** *to hug* **EDDIE**. *She does so, warmly.)*

JILLIAN. It's good to see you. Congratulations on your nomination.

EDDIE. Thanks, Jill.

JILLIAN. Hey, Duncan.

DUNCAN. Hey, Jillian. Hi, Nancy.

NANCY. Gorky. What's a girl gotta do to get a cup of coffee around here?

CYRUS. Oh allow us, Ms. Noble! Please, why don't you all make yourself comfortable.

*(***CYRUS** *indicates they should all take a seat, which they do.* **CYRUS** *begins to pour coffee.* **MAGGIE** *has been staring at the two new arrivals with great interest, to* **NANCY***'s chagrin.)*

NANCY. Take a picture, sweetheart, it will last longer.

MAGGIE. Oh, I'm sorry. I'm sorry. It's just…well, all the gossip pages write about how you two are secretly… you know…*together.*

CYRUS. Margaret O'Leary, you behave!

JILLIAN. It's alright. We've heard it all before.

NANCY. So you like the gossip rags do you, Margaret?

MAGGIE. I do, I confess. And please, call me Maggie.

NANCY. Maggie, huh? Like Maggie the Cat. I like it. Very Liz Taylor.

JILLIAN. You can't believe everything you read in the gossip column, Maggie.

NANCY. Then again, they do get something right every once in a while. *(turns to* **JILLIAN***)* Isn't that right, pet?

JILLIAN. Yes, mistress.

> *(They kiss.* **MAGGIE** *and* **CYRUS** *are gobsmacked.* **EDDIE** *is surprised, but takes it in happily.* **DUNCAN** *shoots out of his chair.)*

DUNCAN. No! For the love of God – stop it!

EDDIE. What's with you?

NANCY. Still got a thing for Jillian, Gorky? Sorry – I don't share. *(turns to* **EDDIE***)* Though I could be persuaded otherwise.

DUNCAN. Stop it! Can't you keep your filthy libido in check? What are you thinking? What if someone is watching?

JILLIAN. I hope they are!

DUNCAN. We're at a funeral, Jill! A man is dead and all you can think about is making a scene.

JILLIAN. I'm sorry, you're right.

NANCY. The fuck he is. This isn't a funeral. I don't see a body, do you?

EDDIE. Now, wait. Duncan's right. We're supposed to be here to honor Dirk. Why don't we all take a moment to do that. Mr. O'Leary, if you could leave us, please.

CYRUS. Of course, Mr. Taylor. We'll be right in the next room if you need anything. Come on, Maggie.

(**CYRUS** *and* **MAGGIE** *exit, leaving the former co-stars alone.*)

DUNCAN. Thanks, Eddie. I knew you'd understand.

NANCY. So what's the deal, Gorczynski?

DUNCAN. Dirk is dead. I thought we all needed a chance to mourn.

NANCY. Yeah, well where the hell is everybody else? Where's his family, his friends?

DUNCAN. His family didn't want any services. But I thought it was important for the four of us to do this together. He was such a big part of our lives. He really touched me, you know? Taught me what it meant to be a decent guy. He showed me that you didn't have to become a Hollywood sell out to be a success. Dirk Howard was the kind of guy who stood by his friends and helped the little guy – just like you said, Eddie – helping us learn our lines and all. I just thought he deserved better than to be written off or forgotten.

EDDIE. It was a good idea, Duncan.

JILLIAN. Very sweet.

NANCY. Bullshit. *(to* **JILLIAN***)* Sit.

(**JILLIAN** *whimpers – happily.*)

JILLIAN. Yes.

NANCY. What's really going on here? Dirk Howard was a washed up stage actor who was just thankful to be collecting a paycheck. And the only reason he ever ran lines with me was to look at my boobs. Not that I cared. And how many times did his script "suggestions" end with him getting a funnier line than you? I'd say about 100% of the time.

JILLIAN. *(meekly)* Still…he was kind of our friend. Or at least a colleague. And he obviously meant a lot to Duncan while he was alive.

NANCY. He's worth a lot more now that he's dead.

EDDIE. What?

NANCY. Why don't you show him the script, Duncan?

DUNCAN. I don't know what you're talking about.

NANCY. I may not be a movie star like Fast Eddie over here, but I've still got a good agent. And she called me two days ago with the word that Duncan Gorczynski has been shopping around an *Oh Spaz* reunion special script from almost the minute Dirk went off the radar.

JILLIAN. You wrote a reunion script?

DUNCAN. Okay. Yes. Yes, I did. But it isn't like what she said. I've had the idea for years. It's just that nobody was interested until Dirk disappeared and stations started repeating the old episodes. And I've got a studio interested – a syndication company. They can package it and sell it to almost any network anywhere in the world. Plus DVD rights, merchandise – even online stuff.

JILLIAN. But why didn't you just call us or our agents?

DUNCAN. I did. God, Jillian, don't you think that was the first thing I did? But none of you call me back. Oh and before you even say you didn't know I called – I'm sure you didn't. You all have "people." "People" and "Agents" and "Managers" and other toadies you pay to make sure you don't have to deal with me.

EDDIE. Come on, Duncan, you know it's not like that.

DUNCAN. Oh yeah, Eddie? Then how is it? If it isn't "like that" than how come this is the only way I could get us all together?

JILLIAN. I can't believe you staged a funeral. That's kind of sick, Duncan.

DUNCAN. You hypocrite. You sit there, all sweet and innocent with your flowery voice, but every sleazeoid website has pictures of you sucking face with Nancy or skinny dipping or walking out of a sex shop with God knows what. And you're calling me sick?

NANCY. Jealous.

EDDIE. Alright. Well, I can see this was a bad idea. Thanks for a great time, Gorky.

(He gets up to go.)

DUNCAN. Wait! Wait! If you'll just read the script. It's good, man. It's REALLY good. Way better than the shit they used to make us say.

(**DUNCAN** *takes the rolled up script out of his suit pocket. It's a wrinkled mess, as if he has been keeping it on him at all times for weeks [which he has].)*

Now, just be careful with it, because it's the only copy I have right now. I mean, there's more on my computer obviously, but I can only print so many free pages a week at the computer warehouse.

EDDIE. *(with sincerity)* Send it to my agent, okay, Duncan? I promise – I PROMISE – will give it a look.

DUNCAN. I don't have that kind of time, man. The studio said they would only do it if we were ALL on board – and on board now. That's why I had to do this. That's why I needed to get everyone together in person, so we could sign something today! Look – look – I know it's all happening really fast. I need you on this one, Eddie. Get my back this one last time. I can't sell it with just me and the girls – they're not exactly family friendly viewing in the eyes of the studio. But you're so famous now…they said they'd do anything you wanted. Maybe if we all just sat down and had a read through. Once you're back in character, it will be impossible to say "no."

NANCY. Eddie's right. Let's blow, Jillian. Follow.

(**NANCY** *starts off, followed by* **JILLIAN**.)

DUNCAN. Think of the fans! Yes! *(calls off)* Maggie? Maggie? Can you come in here?

(**MAGGIE** *re-enters.)*

MAGGIE. Yes, Mr. Gorczynski?

DUNCAN. Maggie, how would you like to be the first person to hear an all-new episode of *Oh, Spaz?*

MAGGIE. Oh, I would just die! Is Eddie going to be in it?

DUNCAN. Of course he is! We're all going to be in it! Isn't that right, Eddie?

EDDIE. Send it to my people, Duncan. Maybe I can do a cameo or something. I have to go.

DUNCAN. You can't go, Eddie.

(EDDIE finally loses his polished cool.)

EDDIE. Look man, this is just plain lame. You staged a funeral to try and broker a TV gig. You know what? You're way more "Hollywood" than I'll ever be, Duncan. Maggie, can you have your brother send me the bill for all of this? Just have him send it to the address on my card.

(EDDIE hands MAGGIE a business card from his pocket.)

MAGGIE. Could you sign it for me, Mr. Taylor? I have a pen.

EDDIE. Sure.

(She pulls out a pen from her hair and gives it to EDDIE who signs the business card.)

DUNCAN. You can't do this, Eddie! People don't want to see me unless I'm playing your sidekick.

EDDIE. Look, I'm sorry, Duncan, that was all a LONG time ago – I'm out. *(turns to leave)* Nancy, Jill – it was great seeing you. Call me if you want tickets to the Globes.

DUNCAN. This is your own fault.

(DUNCAN pulls out a small revolver from his inside suit pocket and points it across the room at EDDIE, who stops dead in his tracks. JILL clings to NANCY. MAGGIE just freezes.)

NANCY. What the fuck are you doing?

EDDIE. Woah, woah – take it easy now, Duncan.

DUNCAN. For ten years, I have watched you get richer, sexier and more famous by the day. First it was the commercials, then the TV shows, then the movies and now the awards. I see your fucking face plastered on every God damn magazine in the grocery market and every piece of shit billboard. For Christ's sake, your face is plastered on the side of my bus! The city bus I use to get to my fucking disgusting job at a computer warehouse.

EDDIE. I had no idea it was that bad for you.

DUNCAN. I tried to tell you! From the minute you arrived… I FUCKING TOLD YOU! You never listened to what I say. Not then and not now.

EDDIE. I'm listening now, buddy. Just tell me what it is you want.

DUNCAN. I already did, Eddie! I needed this reunion special and the only way it was going to happen was with you onboard. There's no way I'm gonna end up like Dirk, okay? I'm fucking BROKE, Eddie – I lost my house, I lost my car – I lost everything. And no one cares. Nobody comes to my stand-up shows and the only time Hollywood calls is if they want me to give an interview about YOU! *(turns gun on* **NANCY***)* Or YOU! *(turns gun on* **JILLIAN***)* Or YOU!

JILLIAN. Duncan, I'll do the special. I think it would be fun.

DUNCAN. Shut up!

*(***DUNCAN*** *fires his gun – narrowly missing* **JILLIAN***.)*

DUNCAN. Nobody wants to hear from a WHORE! *(turns back to* **EDDIE***)* No one was going to care unless Eddie was involved. Too late now I guess, huh? Fuck it. It doesn't matter – I'm getting back on TV one way or another. Something tells me that there'd be a lot of interest in the death of a big time movie star, don't ya think, Eddie?

EDDIE. Don't do anything stupid, Duncan. We can work this out. I'll do the special – maybe I could even talk to my agent about us doing a buddy picture for the summer!

DUNCAN. What?

EDDIE. Sure! Hey – the girls could be in it too. Forget about a reunion special – a whole new movie starring the four of us!

NANCY. We could shoot it in Hawaii!

JILLIAN. Don't you think it's what Dirk would want?

DUNCAN. You're lying.

(He takes aim, cocking the trigger.)

EDDIE. DUNCAN, DON'T!

DUNCAN. Bye bye, Eddie. We're both about to become REAL famous.

MAGGIE. NO!

*(**MAGGIE**, who has been frozen to the spot, dives in front of **EDDIE**, using herself as a human shield.)*

MAGGIE. I won't let you kill Eddie. He's a national treasure.

DUNCAN. What the fuck? Get out of the way! I don't want to hurt you.

EDDIE. Please, Duncan – we can work this out!

MAGGIE. This is just like the end of *Santa Fe Standoff.* You were great in that.

EDDIE. Thanks. Wait – didn't I die at the end of that one?

MAGGIE. Oh. Yeah.

DUNCAN. Sounds like a good one – consider this the superior remake. Now you've got till the count of three to get out of the way or I'll kill the both of you. One…

JILLIAN. Duncan, please!

DUNCAN. TWO

EDDIE. Get out of the way, Maggie!

DUNCAN. THREE

(BANG!)

*(**MAGGIE** falls into **EDDIE**'s arms. A brief moment of shock – then **DUNCAN** falls to the floor dead. **MAGGIE** opens her eyes.)*

NANCY. She's okay!

EDDIE. What the hell happened?

*(**CYRUS** enters, holding a revolver.)*

CYRUS. Everybody okay?

EDDIE. I think so. Maggie, are you okay?

MAGGIE. I must be dead, because I think I'm in heaven.

NANCY. Cyrus, you saved us! How did you know?

CYRUS. Well first off, it was just like Episode 407 of *Oh Spaz* where Duncan held everyone hostage with stink bombs because he wanted to take you to the prom but Eddie had asked you first. I could see it on his face from the moment he walked in. Besides, you were all carrying on so loudly, the stiffs in the other room could hear you.

EDDIE. You're a goddamn hero, Cyrus!

JILLIAN. It was like something out of a movie.

CYRUS. Hero? Little old moi?

MAGGIE. You were so great, Cyrus!

NANCY. You weren't so bad yourself, little lady – jumping in front of the gun like that!

CYRUS. Oh yes, Mags – you were brilliant! I was on the edge of my seat the whole time.

EDDIE. We almost died. He was going to kill us. I would have missed the Golden Globes.

NANCY. Bet you would have won. They ALWAYS give it to you if you die just before the ceremony.

EDDIE. Damn it.

JILLIAN. Where'd you learn to shoot like that, Cyrus?

CYRUS. Clint Eastwood movies.

(He twirls the gun and pretends to holster it.)

EDDIE. You know, Cyrus – I think there would be a lot of interest in this story. How about I set up a little meeting with you and my people – my agent, a couple of writers…this could make a great movie.

CYRUS. A movie about ME?

EDDIE. I could play myself. I'm thinking George Clooney for you.

JILLIAN. Maggie would have to be in it as well. Maggie, I would be honored to play you.

MAGGIE. Oh my goodness – YOU play ME? Of course! You'd be my first choice!

NANCY. This is big. Eddie, what do you say you cancel whatever it is you were going to do today and we have that meeting right now? Before this place is swarming with agents for our new finds.

EDDIE. Good call, Nancy. Why don't you bring your car around and we'll all meet up at my office on Sunset.

NANCY. Jill, let's boogie.

JILLIAN. Can Maggie ride with us?

NANCY. She can do more than that if she's lucky. And well behaved.

MAGGIE. Oh my goodness!

(*JILLIAN takes* **MAGGIE** *by the hand and they follow* **NANCY** *as they exit.*)

(*to* **CYRUS** *as she exits*) I think I just wet my pants again!

EDDIE. You know, I've been reading this script about a mortician who solves crime by day and is a serial killer by night. I would love your insight into the mind of that kind of character. What makes a mortician tick?

CYRUS. Well, of course I consider myself more of an artist than a regular mortician. I like to give the dead a little color, you know? But no matter what, it all starts with a good embalming fluid. Shall we take my car or yours? Oh, listen to me go on – offering a ride to a movie star! This is just the END. The living END!

(*They step over the body of* **DUNCAN** *and exit in conversation.*)

(*Everything dims except a spotlight on* **DUNCAN**'s *body.*)

(*blackout*)

IV.

THE CLIVE WAY

by John P. Dowgin

CHARACTERS

LIONEL – An anger management patient
MICKEY – Same
HAROLD – Same
DOCTOR POOTRAM – Their doctor
CLIVE GARRISON – A motivational speaker
MONOTONE VOICE OVER – Very dry.

PLACE

The Muriel Holbenstein Community Center, Room 137, during the final meeting of The Anger Management Counseling Group.

(In blackness – a voice over a PA system.)

MONOTONE VOICE OVER. Hello, and thank you for calling the Muriel Holbenstein Community Center. The Anger Management Counseling Group, "Why am I Like This: Learning to Coexist with Fury," will have their final meeting this morning at 10:30 in Room 137. Congratulations to all for channeling their threatening tendencies to become productive members of society. Please join us following the meeting for decaffeinated coffee and cake. Also this morning, Clive Garrison, star of the best-selling videos 'Storming to Success' and 'Beat Down their Door the Clive Way' will begin his award-winning lecture series in Room 139. Mr. Garrison's videos, now available in VHS, will be available for purchase at a one-time low price of 67 dollars and 43 cents. *(fade out over the following)* Don't forget to make reservations for next month's Octogenarian Fashion Extravaganza to be held at Mount Airy Lodge…

(Lights up on four men seated in a semi-circle. The **DOCTOR** *sits center.* **HAROLD** *sits to his right. A mannequin is seated to his left.* **MICKEY** *and* **LIONEL** *sit to the* **DOCTOR**'s *left.* **LIONEL** *stands. About 30, he wears a suit.)*

LIONEL. Hi. My name is Lionel, and I was an angry, angry man.

ALL. Hi, Lionel.

LIONEL. My problems started earlier this year when my boss retired, and I really thought I was going to get promoted. But instead they hired some outside guy, and it started off okay. But then he started asking me to work late, come in on weekends. Then he wouldn't let me take the vacation I had requested. And then all

49

these problems cropped up with my expense reports, and he made me give up my office, and then one day I went home early and found him screwing my wife. Just a lot of little shit, really. I bottomed out last December. I was Christmas shopping at FAO Schwartz and I punched out an off-duty toy soldier cause he had the last Furby. So I had to start coming here and I really want to thank you guys because you've helped me see that, well, you know...

DOCTOR. No, no, Lionel, tell us. You have to tell us.

LIONEL. *(parroting just a little)* Uh, that, my anger at my boss was misplaced anger at myself for not doing my job right which is why I didn't get the promotion, and that forces operate on our lives...

ALL. *(repeating their mantra)* ...that are beyond our control.

LIONEL. and my anger was....

ALL. ...depleting my life force.

LIONEL. and that just plain...

ALL. ...Sucked!

LIONEL. That's right. And now I've got a new job. And I just want to say thank you. You guys have really helped me pull my stuff together.

DOCTOR. Good job, Lionel, I have been so impressed with you.

LIONEL. Yeah, yeah, I feel good. And remember if you come in on Thursday, the Blue Light Special is at nine.

MICKEY. *(stands)* Hi, my name is Mickey, and I was an angry, angry man.

ALL. Hi Mickey.

MICKEY. My problem started when I was nine. My family moved and I had to start a new school. The kids there didn't like me cause I was new, and they scared me, and I started to stutter and stuff. And I couldn't lose the stutter, and I would just get madder cause they'd call me cottonmouth or jabberjaw. Then they started calling me Chauncey and that was the worst cause, like, it didn't even make any sense. And this kept up through high school. So the principal saw I wasn't doing so hot and he asked me why. So I told him I couldn't concentrate because I was mad all the time. He asked why, and I told him I was always listening to hear if anyone was calling me Chauncey. And he said that was ridiculous, so I hit him in the face with my Social Studies book. So the cops came, and the judge said I could either go to Juvy or come here every week and I said shit yeah…

DOCTOR. But it was the right choice, wasn't it Mickey?

MICKEY. Oh yeah, cause you know, it helped me see I wasn't really angry at the other kids. I was really angry at my dad because he made me move and he was working all the time, and cheating on Mom with Lionel's wife, which I swear, dude, I knew nothing about…

LIONEL. It's cool.

MICKEY. Yeah, and my anger at him was…

ALL. …beyond my control.

MICKEY. And that was….

ALL. …depleting my life force.

MICKEY. and that just plain…

ALL. …Sucked!

MICKEY. That's right, yeah…and now, the stutter is gone, I'm ready to go back to school a couple of days a week, to a new school, and they're going teach me how to like, build stuff, so that's cool.

DOCTOR. Mickey, you have your entire life ahead of you, son. Say the Mickey's Magic No-Stutter word, Mickey!

MICKEY. *(proudly)* Chrysanthemum! *(sits)*

HAROLD. Okay…

(Stands. He is in his late 20s. He seems to be having more difficulty than the others.)

Uh, my name is Harold, and I was an angry, angry man.

ALL. Hi, Harold.

HAROLD. Um, my problems began about eight years ago, when I graduated from college, and I moved back home. My girlfriend, Ruth, and I were going to save some money and get an apartment, go to graduate school, too. But my mother got very sick, and was confined to a wheelchair. And she needed a lot of help around the house. Ruth got a bit annoyed because of the time mother demanded. And Ruth thought mother was just, you know, faking, that she wasn't sick and just didn't want me to move. And Ruth and I would get into these enormous fights, because sometimes we'd come home and Mom would be vacuuming, and she'd see us and then jump back into the wheelchair and make some noise, like *(imitates a groan)*. And then one day, Ruth and I were supposed to go apartment hunting, but that morning Mom slipped in the shower and thought she'd broken her leg and she needed me to stay. And Ruth went nuts, cause she said a woman in a wheelchair wouldn't even be able to take a shower, and I said well what do you know about it anyway, and so Ruth left and I never saw her again. Later on that day, or it may have been the next year, I asked Mom if she could walk. And she said she could, but then she started crying and said she was feeling better because she had told me, and everything would be okay. And I was okay with that, but I couldn't help but feel that mom had interfered with my personal life. Unnecessarily. And I started fighting with her a lot, and then one day, I saw Dr. Pootram's ad, and I thought it would good for me to start coming here. The police thought so too, and even said they'd pay for it. I guess they were tired of getting called to our house, but anyway it's six years later now and I, um,. I'm feeling…. *(beat)* really, really good!

DOCTOR. That's right, Harold, you made the right call. And now you know your mother was feeling a maternal instinct. And, Harold, together we have investigated the true power of role-play. *(He makes quote marks with his fingers over the technical term.)* Show us.

(HAROLD turns to address the mannequin. What he says he says with great difficulty but total conviction.)

HAROLD. Mother, I need you to know that I was very angry at you for a long time. But it's time for me to move on with my life, and part of that process is accepting that there are forces in my life beyond my control,

(The others stage whisper the mantra along with him.)

and these forces were depleting my life face, and that just….stunk. And I forgive you, mother.

DOCTOR. That was wonderful, Harold. I'm sure that if you were allowed within 500 feet of your mother, she would appreciate your sentiments.

(HAROLD nods.)

Well, these six-months have been tremendously challenging for me. Now, Mr. Shickenfisher from Health and Human Services will be here shortly to run your final test. Once you all pass, which I'm sure you will, I have the honor of advising him to give each of you your 'Anger Buster' certificate *(holds one up for general appreciation)*. You are all now perfectly happy, normal, ambitious and striving young men who can do anything they want. Now I just need each of you to sign the final roll call and… *(searching his pockets)* ,oh…, uh oh, I don't seem to have remembered my pen… Mickey, do you…

(MICKEY shakes his head no.)

Lionel?

(LIONEL checks his pocket and says no.)

Harold?

HAROLD. I'm not allowed to carry pointy things yet.

DOCTOR. Ah, right. Okay, I'll tell you what. Who hasn't finished their energy re-channeling projects yet?

(All raise their hands.)

Okay, take out your projects.

(All reach under the chair and remove a popsicle stick birdhouse.)

DOCTOR. *(cont.)* So finish up your projects and I'm going to go find myself a pen before Mr. Shickenfisher arrives.

(The **DOCTOR** *leaves. The patients work silently on the birdhouses. As the* **DOCTOR** *exits the door,* **CLIVE GARRISON** *enters the hallway. He is wearing an expensive suit and moves with purpose. He carries a case. The* **DOCTOR** *sees him.)*

DOCTOR. Ah, there you are, good!

CLIVE. I know, I know, I'm so sorry I'm running late, traffic is an absolute nightmare...

DOCTOR. Oh, I understand.

CLIVE. They're inside? They're not angry I'm late, are they?

DOCTOR. Oh, I should hope not!

CLIVE. Yes, if they need me, I guess they wouldn't be riled up so easily! *(Both laugh.)*

DOCTOR. Well, you go get things started and I'll be back in two minutes, all right?

CLIVE. Sounds good!

(The **DOCTOR** *leaves.)*

(stops before the door) Room 137? I thought I was in...

(looks at a piece of paper from his pocket)

Damn, Sylvia, I swear to God... I'm getting a Palm Pilot, that's it.

*(**CLIVE** stops, shakes his arms out. **CLIVE** turns and enters the room. He settles himself, removes a bullhorn form his case and speaks into it.)*

ASSHOLES!

*(The three patients almost have a heart attack. They gather themselves and look up at **CLIVE**. They are not sure what to do.)*

CLIVE. *(cont.)* You heard me. *(into the bullhorn again)* Assholes! *(pause)* What are you all looking at? I just walked into a room, look around and called what I saw. *(points at them in turn)* Asshole, Asshole, and Asshole! This room reeks of it. I smell nothing but assholes! Assholes who have been living meek asshole lives, in asshole worlds. Going to asshole jobs, making asshole money, seeing asshole movies and renting asshole videos. Dating asshole women. Driving asshole cars down the great asshole highway on their way to eat at the International House of Assholes and it makes me ill! You make me ill! I see your kind every day and I don't hate you. I pity you. I pity you to the point of pure, unadulterated nausea. I pity you and all of your kind here there and everywhere because it DOESN'T HAVE TO BE THIS WAY!

(Pauses. Assesses his effect. Sees their projects.)

What's with the birdhouses?

HAROLD. *(hides his house)* Are you here to test us?

CLIVE. YES I AM, my asshole friend, yes I am. I have been sent to you on a mission of mercy. You all know who I am and you all need my help…

MICKEY. Aren't you the guy from…

CLIVE. I'M NOT HERE TO TELL YOU WHO I AM, SONNY, I'M HERE TO TELL YOU WHO YOU ARE! I know who I am and I know why I'm here. What I have come to learn, what you can teach me, is who all of you are. Tell me who you are. Because the sooner you open up, the sooner you let me in, the sooner I'1I make you new, improved, and goddammit POWERFUL MODERN MEN. That's who I am, that's what I do, now tell me, who are you?

LIONEL. Lionel.

CLIVE. Good to meet you, Lionel.

HAROLD. Uh, Harold Woodson, sir.

CLIVE. Glad you could make it, Harold!

MICKEY. I'm M,M,... Chrysanthemum! Mickey.

CLIVE. *(regards* **MICKEY** *strangely a second before continuing).* Gentlemen don't think me harsh. Don't think me cruel because I called you all assholes. I could make that same entrance into any apartment, restaurant or day-care center in this great city and be right 99% of the time. You know why? We live in a world inundated by assholes. They surround us. We can't escape them. They steal our air, our water, our parking. And their goal is to prevent our happiness and our self-actualization. But today, I'm going to teach you how to beat them. Let's try an exercise.

(The three students reach for their birdhouses.)

No, no, we'll get those later.

(They put them back.)

I want you all to focus, think back and tell me about the last asshole that affected you personally.

(Long pause. None of them want to answer first.)

MICKEY. Well, um yesterday, I was in Wendy's, and this guy was in line behind me, and I went over to the wall chart to see how much sodium was in the Spicy Grilled Chicken Sandwich. And when I came back, he had cut me.

HAROLD. Whoa.

CLIVE. How did you react to that?

MICKEY. I just called it a force beyond my control.

HAROLD. *(on top)* Beyond his control.

CLIVE. Why did you call it that?

MICKEY. Cause it was.

CLIVE. But what was that your first reaction, Mickey? 'This is a force beyond my control.' Was that your first, primal, cave dweller, homo erectus reaction?

MICKEY. *(pause, while the others look at him curiously)* Yeah, I guess.

CLIVE. *(having retrieved the bullhorn)* BULLSHIT! Harold, tell us about your last asshole.

HAROLD. Um, okay, well, I met this girl at a convention I was at…

CLIVE. Convention, eh Harold?

HAROLD. Yes…at the Klingon exhibit. She was working there. We were talking, and I asked her to go have a drink with me later on. So we were having a very nice time, and then I went to the bathroom. When I got back, there was some guy sitting next to her, in my seat, and he and she were having a very, um, I guess animated would be the word, conversation.

CLIVE. That's a social Hindenburg, my friend. What did you do?

HAROLD. Well, um, let's see, I think I said, um, it was some-thing along the lines of, um…I left.

CLIVE. You left?

HAROLD. Well, it was a force beyond my control, you see.

CLIVE. I see. I see your point. You meet a pretty gal, talk her up, buy her a round and lose her to the first guy with a bigger phaser, is that pretty much it?

HAROLD. Well, that was not my first reaction, but I was able to *(parroting)* channel my initial response into a socially acceptable nullity.

CLIVE. Why don't you tell me your initial reaction, Harold?

HAROLD. *(uncomfortable pause. Then, very quickly)* I'd really rather not say.

CLIVE. Harold, you are a godsend for me. People like you, and like Mickey too. You have the gift. We're going to try an exercise now to capitalize on that gift. It's called a role-play.

(This gets their attention.)

Mickey, stand up. Lionel, just step outside for a second Lionel.

(LIONEL leaves.)

CLIVE. *(cont.)* Mickey, in our minds, we're going to recreate the Wendy's from last night. You're in line, smelling that delectable spicy grilled smell, waiting for the minimum wage counterworker to get the mother with the nine screaming kids their value meals. And you see that nutritional facts chart. And for no reason other than your vast desire to improve your knowledge of worldly things, you wander over to check it out. Now go check it out and send Lionel in.

*(**MICKEY** leaves, **LIONEL** enters.)*

Now Lionel, you come into the Wendy's, and minding your own business you get in line. Now in a second, someone is going to tap you on the shoulder and inform you you've taken his place. This is not the case. You're tired, you're hungry, you've had a long day working at the, where do you work anyway, Lionel?

LIONEL. K-Mart.

CLIVE. No, really. Where.

LIONEL. Really. In Housewares.

CLIVE. Anyway, you've had a long day and you'll be good goddamned if some snot-nosed brat is going to take your spot in line. Okay Mickey, come back in now.

*(**MICKEY** enters.)*

MICKEY. Um, excuse me, I was ahead of you.

LIONEL. No, you weren't.

MICKEY. No, I was. I and, I just went to check out the nutritional fact poster over there. I was only gone a second.

LIONEL. Well, you picked the wrong second, didn't you?

CLIVE. How are you doing, Mickey?

MICKEY. Um, not too good, I think.

CLIVE. How is that making you feel?

MICKEY. Um, *(pause)* okay. I'm okay with it.

CLIVE. But couldn't you really really REALLY go for a Spicy Grilled?

MICKEY. Um….

CLIVE. Biggie-sized?

MICKEY. Well, yeah…

CLIVE. Then keep trying! You're going to let some asshole get between you and your Biggie Fries? How can you lead a satisfied life if you won't even stand up for your own fries?

MICKEY. Um, sir, excuse me, I'm really very hungry and I was in line ahead of you, I swear.

CLIVE. Snot-nosed brat, Lionel. You've been working all day.

LIONEL. Well, I'm sorry, but you left. Life's not fair, sonny, get used to it.

CLIVE. Biggie Fries, Mickey.

MICKEY. But, sir, listen, that's not f… f…fair.

LIONEL. Too bad. I'm just getting a coffee, then I'll be out of your way. Oh, look at that. They're out of coffee. Guess I'm going to have to make 'em brew some….

MICKEY. S…s…sir, please l…l… Chrys…Chry…

CLIVE. How's it going, Mickey?

MICKEY. Bad!

CLIVE. How does that make you feel?

MICKEY. Well…

CLIVE. Happy? Depressed? Sad???

MICKEY. No…

CLIVE. Rhymes with sad?

MICKEY. Yeah…

CLIVE. MAD, Mickey?

MICKEY. Yeah!

CLIVE. And that's what I've come to show you! That's okay!

(All look at him in horror.)

Use that. Use it. Thrive on it! Use the anger to fuel your growth! Fuel your development, your ambition, and your drive for Biggie Fries Mickey!

MICKEY. And that's okay? Really?

CLIVE. You bet, my stammering friend. You bet.

MICKEY. Alright, alright… *(explodes)* Listen, you jobless dick-weed, give me my fucking place back!

HAROLD. Yeah, or what?

MICKEY. Or, I'm g…. g… g…

HAROLD. You're g… g… g… what, huh? What are you g… g… g…

(MICKEY shoves LIONEL. Before LIONEL can react, CLIVE steps in.)

CLIVE. Whoa, whoa whoa, okay!!! Alright Mickey! Way to go, son! A little much, but not bad for a start. We can work with that, temper it a bit, maybe, but good start, good start! The important thing is that you knew what you wanted and you went for it. That's how we need to lead our lives, guys! Not timid, and reserved, and always waiting for 'outside forces' to act on us! Lionel, who was the last asshole to affect you?

LIONEL. My boss. My fucking asshole boss, that's who. Can't even breed right.

(MICKEY gets up but reserves himself. CLIVE does not see this.)

CLIVE. Alright, then let's switch up. Harold, I want you to play Lionel's boss in this role-play. Mickey, sit down. Lionel, step outside. Now Harold, Lionel hasn't been cutting it at work. He's been slacking off, missing deadlines, and soon you're going to have to fire him, all right?

HAROLD. But I could never do that to Lionel.

CLIVE. I'm not asking you to, Harold. It's just an exercise. Lionel, come on in. Now your boss has been under-mining you, hasn't he?

LIONEL. Oh yeah.

CLIVE. He's encroached on your space, right?

LIONEL. You could say that, yeah.

CLIVE. And you deserve things that you're not getting from him, right?

LIONEL. Shit you can't imagine.

CLIVE. Then take a deep breath, go in there, and get what you need.

LIONEL. Sir, we need to speak for a second.

HAROLD. Umm, okay, Lionel. We do need to talk.

LIONEL. Sir, I want my office back.

HAROLD. Well, I can understand that you're upset about that, but…

LIONEL. And I want my vacation time.

HAROLD. I understand, but…

LIONEL. And I want the company car that you drive around like a maniac, and I want you to quit bringing in that brat-ass kid of yours.

CLIVE. Um, Lionel… okay… that's good, but…

*(**MICKEY** moves to the mannequin. Removes its wig and puts it on.)*

LIONEL. *(getting in **HAROLD**'s face)* And for once in your pathetic life, I want you to listen to one god-damned idea of mine because I was doing your job better than you when you were still banging cheerleaders, Chachi!

MICKEY. *(makes a phone sound, then in a woman's voice)* Excuse me, Mr. Boss-man. Lionel's wife is on line two…

LIONEL. *(turns enraged)* COME HERE, YOU LITTLE BASTARD!

MICKEY. She says she needs good bang-bang! *(turns and runs as **LIONEL** chases him around the room)*

LIONEL. I've going to beat you to death with your own teeth, you prick!

MICKEY. Yeah, I'm sh… sh… shaking!!!!!

CLIVE. All right, all right, *(retrieves bullhorn)* ALL RIGHT, NOW! SIT DOWN!

*(**LIONEL** and **MICKEY** sit, but they're not happy about it.)*

WOW! This is the GREATEST CLASS I'VE EVER HAD! Still need a little work on the actual delivery, but the spirit is there! Harold, it's time to talk about you.

HAROLD. I'm sorry, I just really think I should be going home now...

CLIVE. Now Harold, we all have to face up to certain things sooner or later in our lives.

HAROLD. No!!! I'm a perfectly happy normal ambitious and striving young man. I can do anything I want. It's not my fault that these two can't learn a damn thing after six whole months! I'm going to get my certificate and become a productive member of society.

CLIVE. I'm sorry, Harold I don't...

MICKEY. My ass, you damn freak!

LIONEL. Harold, you've got more problems than this whole city put together!

CLIVE. *(trying to regain some measure of control)* You know, I sensed you all may have known each other when I came in this morning...

HAROLD. You two are Neanderthals! There's no helping you! There's never been any hope...

MICKEY. Can it, you weirdo!

CLIVE. You know, the group dynamic between friends can be very effective when combating trouble in our lives...

LIONEL. Yeah, why don't you go home and wheel your crip mother around a little, huh?

HAROLD. Now that's enough! Don't...

CLIVE. In many ways it can be therapeutic for social groups to participate in....

ALL. SHUT UP!

MICKEY. Hey Harold, after six months of your whining, who's a better lay, tell us. Ruthie or Mommy?

HAROLD. *(seething)* Don't say that!

*(**CLIVE** has begun to pack his things rather quickly.)*

LIONEL. Are you kidding? He never had sex with Ruth!

HAROLD. *(steaming)* Don't make me angry...

LIONEL. Aw, Harold's angry! Poor little Harold!

MICKEY. Let Mommy make it all better, Harold!

CLIVE. Now, I'm just going to leave some order forms for my videos on this desk here.

(**HAROLD** *attacks* **MICKEY** *who falls back into the desk* **CLIVE** *is addressing.* **CLIVE** *rather quickly stuffs the aforementioned forms in his sack and leaves.* **MICKEY** *comes after* **HAROLD**, *misses him and shoves* **LIONEL**. **LIONEL** *and* **MICKEY** *begin to wrestle.* **HAROLD** *sees the mannequin and throws it down, choking it.*)

CLIVE. You boys have a good day now! Good work today! Be sure to come again next week when we'll be discussing job interview techniques!

(*As* **CLIVE** *begins to leave, the* **DOCTOR** *reenters.*)

DOCTOR. All set?

CLIVE. I think so.

DOCTOR. Good, good.

(*Reaches into his pocket and hands* **CLIVE** *a wad of bills.*)

CLIVE. Good to work with you again. I think they're ready for another six-month session.

DOCTOR. That's why I keep you on speed dial, Clive.

(*Lights fade as* **CLIVE** *leaves and the* **DOCTOR** *heads back to the classroom*)

End

INTERMISSION

V.

HANGMAN

by Pete Barry

CHARACTERS

DRENTH
YANKUS
TETWILLIGER
HARMON
JONES

SETTING

A classroom at Washington boarding school. Evening.

(Five boarding school students lie strewn about a deserted classroom after hours.)

*(**TETWILLIGER**, the only sober one, holds a pad and pencil, and keeps a small recording device nearby. He observes **JONES** with anticipation, who stares into space, trancelike, unmoving.)*

*(**HARMON** lies passed out on the ground, a vial of dark liquid in his hand.)*

*(**DRENTH** and **YANKUS** share a joint. **DRENTH** sets up a game of Hangman, where **YANKUS** will be the guesser. **DRENTH** draws out five blanks on top of nine, and counts to make sure he is correct.)*

DRENTH. Go.

YANKUS. E.

*(He is correct. **DRENTH** fills the second and third blanks of the first word with the letter E.)*

A.

*(He is wrong. **DRENTH** writes the letter A below the blanks, indicating that it has been used, and draws the base of the gallows. The game continues in this fashion.)*

TETWILLIGER. *(to the unresponsive **JONES**)* I just want to make sure that we're clear on this. You still understand why one of us has to remain sober, and alert. Someone has to be the fully impartial observer.

YANKUS. O.

(Hit. The second and sixth blanks of the second word.)

TETWILLIGER. If I were caught up in the experience that you are right now partaking in, the objectivity of that experience would be lost forever. I might think I had reached some miraculous epiphany, when, actually, my subjectivity would be clouding the fact that my brain was simply not receiving enough oxygen.

YANKUS. I.

(*Miss. The stem of the gallows.*)

TETWILLIGER. I mean, remember when Yankus got stoned and came up with the idea that world peace could be accomplished by creating a machine that would fill the atmosphere with a cloud of marijuana smoke?

YANKUS. Yeah. That was funny.

TETWILLIGER. That was idiotic. But in the moment, he thought he had discovered something profound.

YANKUS. U.

(*Miss. The crossbar.*)

TETWILLIGER. Now, I truly think that you have achieved, with this much more powerful drug, a state in which, at any moment, you might connect with some image of fundamentality, but when that moment comes, one of us must be ready to record, to observe, to impartially decide the merit of that connection. And, while we made a scientifically-based decision that I would be the observer and not the subject, I want you to know that had I lost the coin toss, I would have been fully prepared to sacrifice my own body to this experiment.

YANKUS. B.

(*Miss. The noose.*)

TETWILLIGER. Good. Now. When you said your throat was burning, I took that to be a metaphor. Were you speaking literally?

YANKUS. Q.

(*Miss. The head of the man.*)

TETWILLIGER. Can you hear me?

DRENTH. If there's no U, how could there be a Q?

YANKUS. There's some words like that.

DRENTH. Name one.

YANKUS. I don't know. African words.

DRENTH. You've got a head. Go.

YANKUS. F. For "fuck you."

(Miss. The body. **HARMON** *stirs and rises. He looks around aimlessly for a bit, drinks from his vial, and collapses again.)*

TETWILLIGER. Can you feel your legs?

Because I've read that highs are sometimes accompanied by a loss of bodily sensation.

Which, I suppose, is a kind of ideal Platonism. Freed of the body, that is.

Do you think that Plato ever used hallucinogens? He might very well have approved of their use.

I've really turned around on the issue of drug abuse.

I don't see what the big deal is.

There is quite a lot of scientific and mystical and philosophical exploration still to be accomplished with the use of artificial and natural perceptive supplements.

I mean, obviously we can't have drug dealers running around killing people.

Heroin alone should probably be destroyed and disallowed altogether. The philosophical uses of heroin are at best severely limited.

DRENTH. Go.

YANKUS. S.

(Hit. The fourth and last letters of the second word.)

Colossus? Green Colossus.

DRENTH. Not even close. You should get an arm for guessing.

YANKUS. I didn't tell you to tell me if I was right.

TETWILLIGER. I've also read that banana skins can cause synaesthesia.

YANKUS. L. For "lick my balls."

(Miss. An arm.)

DRENTH. Nope.

TETWILLIGER. You don't hear voices, do you? If you do, they're probably not real. They are most likely hallucinatory. Ignore them, or tell them to find someone else to talk to.

YANKUS. Jesus. What the hell is this?

TETWILLIGER. Do you need to vomit again? Feel free to. I certainly don't want to put any restrictions on you, no matter how revolting. You, after all, would know the path to enlightenment at this stage better than anyone.

YANKUS. Mouse Haus? Doll's house. D.

(Miss. Other arm.)

Is this something I'm not gonna have any way of knowing?

DRENTH. How would I know what you know?

TETWILLIGER. On second thought, perhaps the voices should be treated with a little more attention. An unquestionable, final voice beyond all thought could be just the source we are looking for.

YANKUS. H.

(Hit. The last letter of the first word.)

Oh, you gotta be kidding me. Is this that guy?

DRENTH. What guy?

YANKUS. C.

(Miss. First leg.)

DRENTH. Nope. One more and you're dead.

YANKUS. You don't play with hands and feet?

DRENTH. Nope.

YANKUS. Shit. Let me think.

*(Pause. **HARMON** again rises for a drink.)*

HARMON. *(to **DRENTH**)* When you gave me this stuff to drink. What did you say it was again?

DRENTH. For the fiftieth time. I. Don't. Know.

*(**HARMON** lies down. Pause.)*

TETWILLIGER. If you can speak, I wish you would. This thing we are seeking, call it God, or enlightenment, or Truth – Man has hunted it throughout his mostly barbaric and floundering existence. The largest impediment to his search, I believe, is a lack of communication on the part of the enlightened. For instance, have you ever read the Tao Te Ching? It's supposed to explain the Tao, this same essential pureness in the universe. You know what? You can't understand a fucking word of it. It's a lot of, "the Tao is not things" and "rivers rise up before me, and the people are drowned." Why can't these mystics simply say, in plain Chinese, what the Tao is? Oh, I'm sorry, they say. It's inexplicable. It cannot be put into words. Fine. Show me, then. You can't explain the color red to someone who has never seen it, but you can show them. Just describe a situation, and say, that is Tao. Point to something else, say, that is not Tao. I'll figure the rest out through my own induction.

You're not mad that you lost the coin toss, are you?

I'm sure that if you were, you wouldn't be able to reach any kind of enlightenment anyway. You must open your mind to possibilities. And to others. Open your mind to me. Expose your Self.

I mean, your Self. Don't expose yourself.

Well, of course, again, I don't want to limit you. I mean, if you have to.

Only if absolutely necessary to enlighten me. I mean, I don't want you to. You know.

Let's just drop the whole thing.

Just. Tell me. What springs to your mind? Anything?

Or perhaps nothing springs to mind. Perhaps you have entered a state of no-mind. Nirvana. Beyond thought or consciousness. Zen and Buddhist masters often strive for entire lifetimes to achieve such a state. Isn't it obvious, in this light, the enormous amount of progress the scientific community could offer to the Eastern religions?

TETWILLIGER. *(cont.)* If we could achieve enlightenment, and discover a repeatable method for attaining it?

Six hundred years ago, the masses could not enjoy the information and experience of fine literature simply because the medium, the book, was not accessible to them. Now, with the subsequent advent of technologies, I can download the synopsis to the complete Dante in three seconds. Consumer ready digestible chunks of wisdom. Convenience. That is the bounty of science. So why should we not continue in the great tradition of Gutenberg?

YANKUS. Well, because the height of that guy's movie career was, like, Police Academy Four.

DRENTH. Oh, wait. You know U?

YANKUS. I know I? What?

DRENTH. U. The letter.

YANKUS. I know the letter, yeah.

DRENTH. I think there actually is one.

YANKUS. Oh, man. Where?

*(**DRENTH** fills in the U in the second to last blank of the second word.)*

DRENTH. Oh, yeah. And this is wrong.

(He moves the second O one space to the right.)

YANKUS. You gotta be kidding me.

TETWILLIGER. *(turning to **YANKUS**)* Could you guys be a little happier? You might be causing metaphysical tension.

YANKUS. Man. Well, you owe me a thing. Erase something.

DRENTH. OK. I'll erase his head.

*(He does so. **YANKUS**'s eyes grow wide in epiphany.)*

YANKUS. OH, MAN. Yeah, you gotta do that, cause otherwise, he's already hanging. That's stupid. Who made up this game? The guy's hanging already, before you lose. Right? Like another leg's gonna matter, you can still hang a quadriplegic, right? What a stupid game. Why didn't anybody ever think of that?

TETWILLIGER. That's exactly what I've been saying. By transcending your mundane state of mind, you find enlightenment in other modes of your Being, or perhaps, by stripping away every part of your psyche, attain the ultimate, absolute mode of Being, a Hegelian synthesis of the subject and the object.

(pause)

YANKUS. OK, his head's gone? Good. J.

DRENTH. Nope.

YANKUS. DAMMIT.

*(***DRENTH*** gives the man his second leg.* **TETWILLIGER** *again studies* **JONES**. *Pause.)*

TETWILLIGER. I didn't realize this was going to take so long. Of course, I've never been high on illegal drugs before, I wouldn't know, but I figured you'd have some glimpse of something by now. Even if it was that this whole thing wasn't working. Which would be a great disappointment, but all scientists must be prepared for the possibility. I suppose I should be patient. I mean, if you had achieved the enlightened state by now, obviously, you would have let me know, right?

JONES. No.

(long pause)

TETWILLIGER. No? You mean. No. I. Mm.

(pause)

HARMON. OK. I'm gonna throw up.

(He runs from the room.)

YANKUS. UH. UH. UH. UH. CITIZENS ON PATROL.

DRENTH. You gonna go?

YANKUS. Hold on.

TETWILLIGER. I thought we had agreed.
But, you see, it's that kind of talk that makes me believe you couldn't have found enlightenment. If you had, I can only presume that in the humbling, unfathomable

depth of. I believe that if you had been thrust into the celestial, glowing source of human existence, the Truth revealed would be so enrapturing in its compassion and its full connection to your being, that you would literally have no choice but to allow it to pour outward from your soul and through your lips, to me.

(*pause*)

JONES. Then again, how would you know?

TETWILLIGER. I think you must understand that you have an obligation now. You have a moral obligation to reveal the Truth. I think you owe me the Truth. I mean, I know, had I lost the toss of the coin, I could have easily. I WAS THINKING TAILS, DAMMIT. IT COULD HAVE BEEN ME, IT SHOULD HAVE BEEN ME. I SHOULD HAVE GONE WITH MY INSTINCT. STUPID STUPID ALWAYS THINKING TWICE ABOUT EVERYTHING. ALWAYS THINKING. NO MORE. FROM NOW ON, NO MORE RATIONALITY. FROM NOW ON, IT'S ANIMAL INSTINCT FOR ME.

(*pause*)

YANKUS. You're right. First instinct. P.

(**DRENTH** *makes a buzzer noise. He triumphantly draws the head on the hangman.*)

DRENTH. You lose.

YANKUS. DAMMIT.

DRENTH. Ha ha.

YANKUS. What in freaking hell is this thing?

(**DRENTH** *begins to fill in the letters. He frowns, trying to figure it out. He has spelled out the words TEETH MONSTROUS.*)

DRENTH. Oh. I think I messed it up.

YANKUS. "Teeth monstrous"? What the hell is that?

DRENTH. It was supposed to be teeth *monsters.*

(**YANKUS** *thinks about that.*)

YANKUS. Well, what the hell is that?

DRENTH. You don't remember…oh. Wait. Oh. Oops.

YANKUS. What is it?

DRENTH. I guess. It's nothing. Never mind.

YANKUS. You suck.

TETWILLIGER. *(to* **YANKUS** *and* **DRENTH***)* SHUT UP. *(to* **JONES***)* You are a disgrace to the scientific method. You do realize that you're not going to remember this experience. You'll sink right back into reality, never again to ascend this spiritual peak. By agreeing to be a part of this experiment, you have become a public servant. I demand that you reveal the Truth, if indeed you have stumbled onto any inkling of it. You will give me the Truth. Now. It is your inalienable duty to –

*(***HARMON*** sullenly toddles back into the room. He interrupts* **TETWILLIGER***'s rant.)*

HARMON. Um, guys. I'm not so good.

(Blood trickles, then pours out of **HARMON***'s mouth. He has just enough time to gaze down at himself in shock before he falls to the ground, unconscious.)*

YANKUS. Oh my God.

DRENTH. *(laughing, not comprehending)* Ha.

YANKUS. Holy shit. Holy shit.

TETWILLIGER. You OK? Harmon, you OK? You OK? Holy shit talk to me. Are you OK?

DRENTH. Wait a minute. Is that cranberry juice?

TETWILLIGER. Wait wait wait. *(to* **DRENTH***)* What was he drinking?

DRENTH. Oh my God. I. DON'T. FUCKING. KNOW. Why is everybody always so sure I know what they're drinking?

(During the panic, **JONES** *calmly produces his cell phone and dials three numbers.)*

JONES. Hello. Yes. My friend is vomiting blood. He dropped acid and ingested an unknown substance. I have also been partaking of hallucinogens. The rest of us are stoned. Minus one. Yes? My name is Michael Jones. Yes. No, I'm on a cell phone. At Washington boarding school. Decker building. Room 58. In the basement. I'm not sure. One moment. *(to the others)* Do I require medical attention? *(no response)* I don't think so. I'm just a little happy. All right. Thank you very much. You too. Goodbye.

(He hangs up. Silence.)

DRENTH. We're dead.

YANKUS. Firing squad.

TETWILLIGER. WHAT THE HELL IS WRONG WITH YOU? Why did you have to tell them we were doing drugs?

JONES. It was the truth.

(blackout)

VI.

TRICKS OF THE TRADE

by John P. Dowgin

CHARACTERS

EDDIE, a business man
RALPH, same
A VISITOR

PLACE

An office, late at night.

(An office. A few desks, a couple of chairs. Dark.)

(Offstage, **EDDIE** *and* **RALPH** *can be heard, singing very badly off-key, approaching…)*

EDDIE & RALPH. Show me the way to go home/I'm tired and I want to go to bed/I had a little drink about an hour ago/and it gone right to my head…

*(***EDDIE*** and **RALPH**, *both thirties, both plastered, stagger into the office.* **EDDIE** *starts to make beeping sounds.* **RALPH** *continues to sing…)*

RALPH. Wherever I may roam/by land or sea or foam/you can always hear me singing this song…

EDDIE. And then the shark starts to bump the side of the boat…

RALPH. And they start to drop out…first Quint…

EDDIE. Then Hooper

RALPH. And Brody last, cause what the fuck does he know…

(They start to hum the Jaws theme.)

EDDIE. Greatest movie ever.

RALPH. I don't know about that…

EDDIE. Bullshit. Greatest movie ever.

RALPH. The Godfather. Lawrence of Arabia. Casablanca…

EDDIE. Jaws. Not a wasted fucking frame.

RALPH. Whatever you say.

EDDIE. Whatever I say. What a wonderful philosophy you have.

(They look at each other, smiling.)

RALPH. We did it.

EDDIE. You did it.

RALPH. We did it.

EDDIE. You.

RALPH. Not really.

EDDIE. Fuck not really. We tried.

RALPH. No...

EDDIE. For seven years, we tried. You did.

RALPH. That's not fair.

EDDIE. Fuck fair, it is what it is.

RALPH. Seven years of trying laid the groundwork for what I did.

EDDIE. That's not what I heard.

RALPH. You heard wrong.

EDDIE. Bullshit. I heard from Ken.

RALPH. From Ken?

EDDIE. From Ken.

RALPH. Fuck.

EDDIE. He said for the past six months, you've been a different guy.

RALPH. Ken said that?

EDDIE. Ken said that.

RALPH. Fuck.

EDDIE. Fuck right. Look, Lempshire, those bastards, they've been dicking us over ever since we took them on as a client. Right?

RALPH. Right enough.

EDDIE. They've been, OK, absolutely fucking tea-bagging us on contracts for seven years, ever since we signed them.

RALPH. More fucking trouble than they were worth.

EDDIE. Fucking us over every time we talked about extending their contract. Give an inch, take a mile. Then, all of a sudden, six months ago, you walk into that board room. And you don't just start pitching them new software. You don't just start pitching them upgraded software. Out of the clear blue sky, you start pitching them the extended warranty along with it all...Ken said you were like...

RALPH. I…I don't know.

EDDIE. Fuck, he said he didn't even know you. You were like…a new man.

RALPH. I just figured things needed a change.

EDDIE. Fucking A they needed a change.

(They drink, look at each other.)

EDDIE & RALPH. Nine hundred thousand a year for five years!

EDDIE. I can't even get my head around it.

RALPH. I know.

EDDIE. Could you even imagine those numbers three years ago!

RALPH. I know.

EDDIE. I can't!

RALPH. I know!

EDDIE. It's not like we even gave them anything new!

RALPH. I know!

EDDIE. Unfuckingbelieveable. How'd you do it?

RALPH. No...

EDDIE. I gotta know how you did it. I do.

RALPH. No…

EDDIE. Yes. I gotta know how you did it.

RALPH. No, you don't.

EDDIE. I do.

RALPH. No, no, don't worry about it. Come on. What are you going to do with it?

EDDIE. With what?

RALPH. Your bonus.

EDDIE. Oh, I haven't even thought of…

RALPH. Bullshit, you haven't.

EDDIE. No, I haven't thought about it.

RALPH. Whatever.

EDDIE. Yeah? What are you going to do with yours?

RALPH. I…. I dunno. I, uh, I haven't thought about it.

EDDIE. Want another drink?

RALPH. Does the pope shit in the woods?

(**EDDIE** *digs in his desk and produces a bottle of Dom Perignon.*)

EDDIE. Am I the best or am I the best? That's not a trick question.

RALPH. The fuck did you get that?

EDDIE. Been saving it.

RALPH. In your desk.

EDDIE. For a special occasion.

(*pop*)

RALPH. Ah, fucking music to drunkass ears.

(**EDDIE** *pours. They toast. Beat.*)

EDDIE. Come on! How'd you sell them? How'd you –

RALPH. No!

EDDIE. Every year we'd march into their office.

RALPH. Like clockwork.

EDDIE. Like lemmings.

RALPH. Fucking futility defined.

EDDIE. Until this year.

RALPH. It's pretty sweet!

EDDIE. Fuck sweet! It's Godiva! *(They toast.)* You know what? It doesn't matter how you did it.

RALPH. No.

EDDIE. You did it.

RALPH. I did – We did. I'm sorry…

EDDIE. No, no…

RALPH. No, that's dick of me.

EDDIE. It isn't.

RALPH. It is. We did it.

EDDIE. No.

RALPH. Yes.

EDDIE. No! No, Ralph, you did it! You went in there and you sold them.

RALPH. Maybe. But…

EDDIE. Fuck but.

RALPH. No, no, you can't fuck but, Eddie.

(EDDIE breaks into hysterics.)

RALPH. What?

EDDIE. You said fuck but.

RALPH. You're drunk.

EDDIE. You're not?

(EDDIE dials his cellphone.)

RALPH. Who you calling?

EDDIE. Ken was supposed to meet us at the bar.

RALPH. He was?

EDDIE. Yeah. Didn't he tell you?

RALPH. I haven't talked to him since Wednesday.

EDDIE. *(beat)* What?

RALPH. What what? I haven't talked to him since Wednesday.

EDDIE. All right, settle down, it's not the… *(beep)* Ken, it's Eddie. We left the bar, we're back at the office. Get over here, you lameass, this is your party, too. *(hangs up)* Anyway.

RALPH. Anyway.

EDDIE. All right, anyway. I'm going to pay off my credit cards.

RALPH. What?

EDDIE. With the bonus. I'm gonna pay off my credit cards.

RALPH. Oh. OK. Cool. Smart. Then? *(silence)* Oh. Oh.

EDDIE. Shit got rough, man. It got tight.

RALPH. Wow, man, that's…the whole bonus?

EDDIE. Yeah.

RALPH. You should've…

EDDIE. Look, I don't want to talk about it, OK?

RALPH. OK, but, fuck man, if you needed …

EDDIE. I didn't need help. We got by. OK?

RALPH. OK, but…

EDDIE. No buts. It's OK. And you did help me. You sold five years for nine hundred thousand. The bonus is saving my fucking skin. OK?

RALPH. OK, man. I'm sorry, I shouldn't have reacted that way.

EDDIE. *(pours them a drink)* It's OK. You asked me a question, I answered it, you reacted how you reacted. Nothing to get upset about. Not tonight. *(They toast.)* Now you tell me.

RALPH. What?

EDDIE. You asked me a question…

RALPH. No, man…

EDDIE. I answered. I asked you a question…

RALPH. Listen…

EDDIE. I don't know what you're afraid of.

RALPH. What's your favorite movie?

EDDIE. Are you drunk or stoned? We talked about Jaws all the way back from the fucking bar…

RALPH. All right, exactly. And if Jaws, as a movie, loses steam at any point...

EDDIE. It doesn't.

RALPH. OK, if there's one disappointing moment…

EDDIE. There isn't.

RALPH. But if there were…

EDDIE. It's when the shark appears.

RALPH. Exactly. Why?

EDDIE. Cause you built it up so much in your head, it can't meet your expectations.

RALPH. So stop fucking asking me how I did it.

EDDIE. What are you so afraid of, man?

RALPH. *(beat)* Thank god it's Friday.

EDDIE. It's Saturday now.

RALPH. You know what I mean.

EDDIE. Hey, I forgot to tell you. Ken and me rented a boat for Sunday. Blues are running down just south of Lavallette. You in?

RALPH. Oh. No, no, that's OK.

EDDIE. What?

RALPH. I don't want to go.

EDDIE. Get the fuck out of Dodge.

RALPH. Consider me out of Dodge.

EDDIE. You're turning down a fishing trip?

RALPH. I'm not up for it.

EDDIE. OK.

RALPH. What?

EDDIE. Nothing, it's just…

RALPH. Just what?

EDDIE. It's not like you to turn down a fishing charter.

RALPH. I'm just not up for it.

EDDIE. OK. OK. All right.

(*They drink.* **EDDIE** *smiles,* **RALPH** *is staring off into space.*)

RALPH. It's pretty good.

EDDIE. Yeah, yeah…Ken's right.

RALPH. Hm?

EDDIE. Something's up with you, man.

RALPH. Ken said that?

EDDIE. Ken said that.

RALPH. Ken's a smart guy.

EDDIE. God dammit, Ralph, you can't fucking do this to me!

RALPH. What do you mean?

EDDIE. *(throws* **RALPH** *his phone)* That text. Read it. This afternoon. "Just talked to Ralph. Meet me 30 early at the bar." Why would Ken ask me to get to the bar a half hour before we were supposed to meet you there? Huh? Why would he do that? And why would you lie about talking to him today?

RALPH. I have no fucking idea. I haven't talked to Ken in…

EDDIE. You can't shitcan me! Not now, you can't, please, I'm begging you!

RALPH. Eddie, what the fuck…

EDDIE. I know I haven't sold anything in two years, the market's been cold as shit, but for fucks sake, please, not now! Ralph, please, I'm begging you! As a friend, as your colleague for, for, for eleven fucking years, as a human goddamn being, please…

RALPH. Eddie, what do you think is going on here?

EDDIE. Ralph, come on! You've made the sale of the century, Ken's about to come out with a new release of the software, you're a two man fucking wrecking crew and you don't fucking need me any more!

RALPH. Eddie, relax, you're drunk, OK?

EDDIE. Of course I'm drunk, I'm about to be out of a job! That's what you do when you're out of a job!

RALPH. Eddie, I'm not going to fire you. OK? Ken's not going to fire you, nobody's…that's not what Ken wants to talk to you about.

EDDIE. Bullshit.

RALPH. Relax.

EDDIE. What did Ken want to talk to me about, Ralph?

RALPH. Sit down. Sit. Sit down.

EDDIE. I'm sitting.

RALPH. You're hovering. Sit.

EDDIE. OK. Better?

RALPH. Yes. Much. OK. Now…we have to lay some ground rules for this here discussion we're about to have.

EDDIE. Ground rules.

RALPH. Yes. Rules. Of the ground. They're simple. Do you agree to them?

EDDIE. You haven't told me what they are yet.

RALPH. Doesn't fucking matter. I want to know if you agree to them. Otherwise this conversation proceeds directly to sports scores and weather.

EDDIE. OK.

RALPH. OK. First, you repeat what I'm about to tell you to no one.

EDDIE. No one.

RALPH. Not Ken. Not Marjorie. Not the Pope. You don't whisper what I'm about to tell you under your breath to yourself. Second. You make no value call on what I'm about to tell you.

EDDIE. Value call?

RALPH. You will not judge me based on what I'm about to tell you.

EDDIE. How can I reasonably promise that?

RALPH. Figure it out on your own time.

EDDIE. OK. OK. I promise.

RALPH. All right. All right. Let's go back six months.

EDDIE. Six months?

RALPH. June the sixteenth. A Monday. It's night, and I can't fucking sleep cause I have to be up at six o'clock in the fucking morning to get on a train to Greenwich fucking white bread Connecticut to go talk with fucking Lempshire. I'm staring through sweat at my clock thinking, "If I fall asleep right now, I'll get seven hours of sleep." Before I know it, I'm staring at midnight and recalculating. "If I fall asleep right now, I'll get six hours of sleep." Pretty soon it's five, and pretty soon it's four. And pretty soon after that I realize fuck, if I fall asleep now, I'm going to miss the fucking train, I'm so fucking exhausted. And I realized that's exactly what I wanted. To miss the meeting. No, no, more than that…I couldn't go. If I had to get up and get on that train, my body would go into a complete state of shutdown, I'd curl up into a fetal position right on the train platform if I had to go sit in that board room with those mother fuckers. I knew it. So I got up, got dressed, walked out of my apartment.

EDDIE. At…two in the fucking morning?

RALPH. Two twenty three.

EDDIE. Where…

RALPH. Anywhere. Anywhere that wasn't normal, anywhere that wasn't me. Started walking uptown. Before I knew it, I was at Columbus Circle. And all the while I'm walking I'm thinking, I've been doing this for seven years. I've been selling this same software for seven years, I've been talking to these same clients, or ones just fucking like them, every day for seven years. That's three hundred and sixty five times fucking seven, and I started trying to do the fucking math in my head, and I couldn't figure out which five I needed to carry where and all of a sudden I realize I must've made a left at some point, cause I'm in the middle of fucking no-man's land somewhere the fuck between ninth and tenth. So I stopped. I sat down right there, right where I was, two feet from a puddle of piss, but I didn't fucking care and I made a decision. I wasn't going to move until I figured out what was in my head. I went over it time and time again. I'd think about my meeting with Lempshire last year, the year before that, trying to figure out what was different, what was it about this time, this meeting, that was driving me out of my fucking skull. There was nothing. And then it hit me. That was it. Exactly fucking it. Nothing about this meeting was going to be different than any other meeting I'd gone to in the last seven god damned years. And if that wasn't bad enough, my mind chose this moment to come unhitched from whatever rusty chain had tethered it to sanity, and when it struck bottom it exploded into the reality that my job is to sell…nothing. Nothing real. I sell software. Electrons. Little bits of subatomic matter that someone promises me are arranged in a unique pattern on an electrosensitive media that do something special when you smack them with other electrons coming from other electrosensitive media. And someone gives me money to do this. Someone thinks this pursuit justifies financial compensation. And I couldn't deal with this. I realized…a man can only sell nothing for so long before he just gets pissed. And twenty plus years of emotion welled up and I just became this conduit of rage seeking an outlet. And then I found it.

EDDIE. You…

RALPH. He asked me for change.

EDDIE. He…he asked you for…wait, who?

RALPH. "Mister, got any change?" he asked. I realized I'd been sitting next to him for however long I'd been sitting there. Some wino. Probably the source of the Yellow River next to me. Change, he asked me for. I'd just realized nothing in my life had changed for twenty years and this mother fucker asks me for change?

EDDIE. Ralph…he didn't mean…

RALPH. I know that now, Eddie! For Christ's sake, I'm not an idiot. But in that moment…it was so clear…so…

EDDIE. So…

RALPH. I killed him.

EDDIE. You…

RALPH. I killed him.

EDDIE. *(after a long pause)* Go on.

RALPH. Once it was done…I went home.

EDDIE. You went home.

RALPH. I walked in the door, it was about five. I had an hour to shower, get dressed, make it to Grand Central in time to get to Greenwich.

EDDIE. OK. You seem to have left a little something out of this. You killed a man.

RALPH. Yes.

EDDIE. With your bare hands?

RALPH. A wino. Not exactly a physical specimen.

EDDIE. And then you walked home. And an hour later you got on a train to Greenwich, walked into a board room, and made the sale of a lifetime.

RALPH. Bingo.

EDDIE. No. No. Bingo is something you say when you have five little tiles in a row....

RALPH. I asked you not to make a value judgment...

EDDIE. I'm not! I'm not...

RALPH. Eddie. My friend. All of my professional life, I've made no difference. Maybe I sold something to someone, but even then, what happened? Some money went from one bank account to another, some electrons went from one office to another. What's that? Turbulence. A bump in the universe soon negated by a bump in the other direction. Nothing I ever did mattered. But when I grabbed that useless, piss-stained fuck by the throat, and when I squeezed...I expected him to fight me. You know? I expected resistance, a kick to the balls, a scratch to the eyes, something, anything, like you'd like to think you'd do in his place. But I think he was too shocked. You know? By the time reality set in, it was too late. I squeezed. And tissue, his trachea, his esophagus, just...collapsed under my fingers. Then...I heard it, I swear I did, just the faintest little...'pop'. I did some googling when I got home that night, I think it was his larynx. And you know, he just...sank. I'd...I'd done something that everyone, all my life, had told me would be unthinkable. Suddenly selling the extended warranty didn't seem so hard.

EDDIE. *(a long pause)* I'm going to make a value judgment here.

RALPH. Yeah. So did Ken.

*(A pause. **EDDIE** dials the phone. It rings...and rings... and rings.)*

EDDIE. Ralph.

RALPH. Eddie.

EDDIE. Ralph.

RALPH. Eddie.

EDDIE. *(puts down the phone)* When did you tell this to Ken?

RALPH. Yesterday.

EDDIE. Yesterday?

RALPH. Yesterday. Like today, but gone.

EDDIE. And…Ken…He…made a value judgment?

RALPH. Although I'd explicitly asked him not to.

EDDIE. Ralph…did you…did you kill Ken?

RALPH. I'm not going to tell you that. What do you think, I'm fucking crazy?

EDDIE. OK. OK. OK. I…OK. I promised you that I would not…judge you about this.

RALPH. That's right. You did.

EDDIE. I did. So I won't. Judge you, I won't, I won't judge you, OK?

RALPH. I'd hope not.

EDDIE. OK…OK…how about we discuss this rationally?

RALPH. Love to.

EDDIE. OK. Killing someone…taking another human life, is…it's…

RALPH. You can't say that it's wrong.

EDDIE. Actually, I can.

RALPH. You can't. That assumes foreknowledge of all potential consequences of the action.

EDDIE. You're going to have to wind that one back for me.

RALPH. This bum that I killed. Let's say later this week, he stumbles drunk into the street. And let's say there's a car gonna hit him. Driver's a young woman. Young pregnant woman. And in her panic, in her instinctive reaction to avoid hurting this man, she plows into a streetlamp, wraps her little sedan around a hunk of metal, splatters herself all over the street. That's two lives. Two lives wasted because of this…person.

EDDIE. Now who's assuming foreknowledge of outcomes?

RALPH. I'm not assuming it. You said killing a person was bad. I just gave you an example to the contrary.

EDDIE. Fine. Who's to say he doesn't get hit by that car. End up in Mount Sinai for three weeks. Dries out. Gets a good doctor. Someone who doesn't judge him. He gets out of that hospital, learns to drive an ambulance. Learns it well. Saves a couple dozen people he does it so well. In that iteration, you've killed a couple of dozen people. Plus one.

RALPH. OK. How about this? I kill a man living on the street. It gives me the confidence to go make the sale of a lifetime the next morning. This sale of a lifetime puts my sales group in its top annual percentile. Means the top annual bonus. Means one member of my team can pay off his credit cards.

EDDIE. Ralph…

RALPH. Can you pay off your debts because I killed this man? Yes or no?

EDDIE. Yes.

RALPH. And is that good or bad?

EDDIE. That's…immaterial.

RALPH. Look. Follow me here. You say taking a life is wrong. I say it's not. We just agree to disagree about this, we can go on like nothing ever happened, OK?

EDDIE. No, Ralph. I'm sorry. I can't ignore this. If you have to fucking kill me because of that, then fucking kill me. Go ahead and kill me. Like you killed Ken.

(KEN enters.)

RALPH. Hey, Ken.

KEN. Hey, guys. Sorry I'm late. Got a flat on the FDR, I go to dial AAA and I realized my phone was dead. Fucking disaster. Anyway. Fuck, did I walk into a funeral?

EDDIE. Ken….

KEN. Yeah, Eddie?

EDDIE. You're…

KEN. I'm fucking starving is what I am.

RALPH. How about we head on out for some Tapas?

KEN. Sure, Ralph, sounds great.

EDDIE. I'm…no, I'm sorry, I'm gonna go home, guys.

KEN. Eddie? You OK?

EDDIE. No. No, Ken, I'm really not…

KEN. Eddie, sit down. Before you go, we've got to talk about something. Something serious.

EDDIE. Um. OK, but maybe we should…

KEN. Should what?

EDDIE. *(whispering)* Ken, maybe we should talk about this… later. Alone.

KEN. Oh. No, no, no, this, um, this concerns Ralph, too.

EDDIE. I know it does…

KEN. Sit, Eddie.

EDDIE. Ken, we…

KEN. Eddie. Sit. Please. *(EDDIE sits.)* Eddie, you've…Fuck. Fuck, I don't know how to say this…

EDDIE. Ken?

KEN. Eddie…I'm going to have to let you go.

EDDIE. What?

RALPH. What?

KEN. I'm sorry, Eddie. You just…you haven't been pulling your weight. Not for a long time.

EDDIE. Ken, none of us have been pulling our weight for a long, long time…

KEN. I'm sorry, Eddie.

EDDIE. Ken…Ken, look, you…I haven't told anyone else but you about Marjorie…

KEN. I know you haven't. Look, this was the hardest decision I've ever had to make, Eddie…

EDDIE. She's…she's not through it yet. Her oncologist says she's got…her chances aren't even thirty…You cut me off now…oh, fuck, Ken, you cut me off now, I'm going to lose my insurance…

KEN. No, no, you can COBRA your benefits through…

EDDIE. With what, Ken? Do you know how much COBRA costs! I…my credit cards are already maxed cause of the fucking specialists…

RALPH. Eddie, Marjorie's sick?

EDDIE. Yes! Yes, Ralph, she is, why the fuck do you think I'm so maxed on my…. Ken, please, you can't do this.

KEN. Eddie, I have to. Ralph's sale buys us some time to reorganize. I have to start making cuts now in case we have to weather any more downturns.

RALPH. Marjorie's…she's sick?

EDDIE. And you're firing me? You're firing me? You're keeping him but firing me?

KEN. Of course, Eddie, Ralph just closed Lempshire on extended warranty! Nine hundred thousand a year for five fucking years!

EDDIE. Did he tell you how? Did he tell you how he closed the Lempshire deal?

KEN. Of course! That's the kind of man I need on this sales team, Eddie. Stone cold, ruthless bastards.

(**RALPH** *wraps his arm around* **KEN***'s neck and strangles him to the ground.* **EDDIE** *watches* **KEN***'s body grow lifeless, then collapse in* **RALPH***'s arms.* **RALPH** *steps away.*)

RALPH. Marjorie's a good person.

EDDIE. Now what?

RALPH. Last time I just left.

EDDIE. That won't work this time.

RALPH. Yeah. Is that fishing boat on Sunday in your name or his?

EDDIE. Mine.

RALPH. Good.

(*beat*)

EDDIE. Thank you, Ralph. (*beat*) What do we do till Sunday?

RALPH. Wait.

EDDIE. (*beat*) What do we do after Sunday?

RALPH. You tell me.

EDDIE. Well. (*beat*) There's next week's follow-up with Lempshire to prep for.

(*blackout*)

VII.

THE BANDERSCOTT

by Pete Barry

CHARACTERS

BOB HENDERSON
EILEEN
HARCOURT McALLISTER
DR. THINN
TERRY
WARREN
VARIOUS ASSISTANTS

SETTING

Bob's office. Present day.

PRODUCTION NOTES

Terry's team can be composed of any number of members. The more, the funnier. If performed as a part of "Accidents Happen", the cast of "The Clive Way" can enter with the rest of the team during the final confrontation, still fighting each other.

Typically, the actor who plays Warren doubles as Eileen's voice, though the part can be played by an offstage actress.

In the Porch Room's productions, we have never managed to get anything that looks like a live octopus, and suggest the closest possible substitute. We do not advocate using a real octopus. It will die, messily.

*(**BOB HENDERSON** argues away over the phone in his office.)*

BOB. No, I think the product has potential. Yeah. And at that price, who wouldn't want one? No, sir, I completely understand where you're coming from, I mean, that's why we offer these alternative broadcast services. Think about dominoes. Who would have ever bought that game if someone hadn't realized how much fun knocking a few over could be? You know? Right. So I think it just needs a little more work before we give it more airtime. Well, yes, lower injury statistics would probably help. Right. But we have your number, we'll be in touch. Right I gotta go now. I have an appointment. Right. *(**BOB** rolls his eyes.)* All right, then, tell him he can see me later. Yes. OK. Mm-hm. OK. Bye.

(He hangs up the phone. He calls through the half-open door.)

BOB. Eileen?

EILEEN. *(**EILEEN** calls from the other room.)* Yes?

BOB. Can we murder Warren Edds? Take a contract out on his life, or something?

EILEEN. I'll check the Yellow Pages, sir.

BOB. Don't get me wrong, his infomercials are selling off the charts, but where does he find these clients? These products get more ridiculous every day.

EILEEN. He'll sell them, though.

BOB. I know! I can't understand it. And his pitch is so corny – he's like a throwback to 1960 and Ron Popeil. But it works. He once got interviewed on Sixty Minutes and sold the host his own tie for twenty bucks. You know how he got his start? Selling double-sided toothbrushes. Double-sided! Who invented that? And Warren sold a hundred million units.

EILEEN. He's got a scary amount of talent.

BOB. You know he's reached the level of Nostradamus in the tabloids? I saw one today actually proclaim him the messiah. And people believe it. You know what, cancel that assassination. I don't want to start a religious war.

EILEEN. I'm already on it, sir. Should I let in your 10 o'clock?

BOB. Hm? (**BOB** *checks his appointment book.*) Oh. I actually do have an appointment. Great. Yes, who is this again?

EILEEN. Mr. McAllister, sir.

BOB. Um. Sure. Send him in.

> (**BOB** *quickly makes himself presentable. A moment later,* **HARCOURT McALLISTER**, *a large smiling Texan, strolls through the door, accompanied by* **DR. THINN**, *a strange and nervous little man.* **DR. THINN** *carries a briefcase.*)

BOB. Mr. McAllister?

McALLISTER. That's my name. You can call me Harcourt, though, Mr. McAllister's my father, bless his soul.

BOB. Hi. I'm Bob Henderson, I'm the head of our distribution. This is?

McALLISTER. Oh, this is Dr. Thinn, Doctor, Mr. Henderson.

BOB. Call me Bob, please.

> (**BOB** *extends his hand;* **THINN** *does not take it. He seems to regard everything in the room with a kind of numb horror.*)

McALLISTER. You'll have to excuse him, he's a little jet-lagged. We just got in from Texas.

BOB. One of my favorite states.

> (**BOB** *closes the door behind them.*)

McALLISTER. So, my father always said, don't dilly-dally, son, show the man what you're here for. You want to see the product.

BOB. I can't wait to.

> (**THINN** *draws from his briefcase a small, sleek and silver object, a little longer than a ballpoint pen. On one end*

sprouts a small round bulb, electric red. **McALLISTER** *takes it and displays it proudly.)*

McALLISTER. This, Bob, is the Banderscott. *(slight, dramatic pause)* Now, before you say anything about it, I want you to know what you get when you buy one of these beauties.

BOB. Well, it might help me if I knew what it does.

*(**McALLISTER** reaches into **THINN**'s briefcase and pulls out a small jet black box.)*

McALLISTER. Now, first off, you get convenience. Look at the size of this thing. Look at it, Bob.

*(He hands the Banderscott to **BOB**.)*

This little darling can fit right in your coat pocket, purse, anywhere! It's so convenient to carry around, you have no excuse not to have one with you at all times. And it comes in a stylish and convenient carrying case!

*(**THINN** pulls a plush bag out of his briefcase and offers it to **BOB**. **BOB** begins to study the Banderscott. He lightly moves a finger towards the red bulb. This alarms **DR. THINN**.)*

THINN. Ooh, don't touch that end.

*(**BOB** pulls his finger away before touching it.)*

BOB. Oh. Fragile, is it?

McALLISTER. Not at all, Bob! Matter of fact, that's another great piece of news – this puppy is totally indestructible. Now, I know you've sold products like those knives, the ones they say "never break"? Hell, Bob, I tried to use 'em on diamonds, they dulled after three or four. You gotta check the quality of your merchandise. But that boy who sells 'em, I love him! He's a genius! What's his name?

BOB. Warren Edds.

McALLISTER. Warren Edds! Yeah! Aw, I'd be bowled over backwards if he signed on for our commercial. Is he available?

BOB. I'll check. Can I ask what the Banderscott actually does?

McALLISTER. Well, tell Warren this, Bob, when I say indestructible, I mean totally indestructible. We have footage from when we strapped one of these to the shuttle launch platform. It came out better than ever, all shinied up, too!

BOB. That's very impressive. Does it –

McALLISTER. Would you buy that for three hundred dollars, Bob? That kind of indestructibility?

BOB. That depends on what it –

McALLISTER. How about two hundred dollars? I can see you're a hard sell. Ninety-nine dollars.

BOB. Does it do anything?

McALLISTER. Oh, but, wait, I almost forgot.

(He obviously has not, for he now proudly displays the black box.)

Not only do you get this unbelievable little device – but you also get –

(He pulls open the box, revealing nicely arranged silverware)

– a hand crafted sterling silver spork set!

BOB. Sporks.

McALLISTER. Yeah, you know, those spoon-fork thingies, ain't it great, nobody's got these in silver, it's a totally original selling point!

BOB. I see. Mr. McAllister.

McALLISTER. Harcourt.

BOB. Harcourt. What does it do?

McALLISTER. The spork set?

BOB. The Banderscott.

McALLISTER. Oh, the Banderscott.

BOB. Yes. What does it do?

McALLISTER. It kills people. And it comes with a full money-back guarantee!

(beat)

BOB. It what?

McALLISTER. But why pay ninety-nine dollars for all this, when we'll give it to you for seventy-five dollars? Still not satisfied?

BOB. Harcourt!

McALLISTER. Hm?

BOB. It?

McALLISTER. What?

BOB. What did you say it does?

McALLISTER. Kills people.

(long pause)

BOB. It kills people?

McALLISTER. Ain't it a beaut? The body, what the Doctor calls the casing, is titanium, don't that sound heavy? It's light as a pen!

BOB. Mr., Mr. McAllister.

McALLISTER. And it's made with the simplest materials, totally recyclable, if you could recycle it. But who'd want to recycle one of these beauties anyway?

BOB. Mr. McAllister.

McALLISTER. Oh, wait, I should show you what we plan to do on the commercial. We got most of it planned out, but we're still working with the ad agency.

(He opens the door, not looking out. Enter the ad agent, **TERRY,** *followed by a* **LARGE TEAM OF PRODUCTION ASSISTANTS,** *who begin setting up a table, a presentation board, and a plethora of AV equipment. They drag a twisted mess of extension cords behind them.)*

TERRY. Mr. Henderson.

McALLISTER. Bob.

TERRY. Bob. Our preliminary tests show that the key demographics we should be looking at are senior citizens, i.e., sixty-five plus, and unmarried upper-lower and lower-middle class mothers.

*(They set the television down on **BOB**'s desk. One **ASSISTANT** wields an enormous sledgehammer, and another holds down a live octopus. **BOB** is aghast. **THINN** has crumpled in the corner of the room, like a small child.)*

BOB. Hold on, hold on!

TERRY. Also, thanks to recent studies in color-indexing and subliminal cues, we've provided quite a substantial amount of psychologically conducive colors to the overall scheme of the background in the advertisement.

LEAD ASSISTANT. Audio's all hooked up.

TERRY. Go.

*(Deafening roar. **McALLISTER** yells over the noise.)*

McALLISTER. That's from the footage of the shuttle launch! Not a mark on it!

BOB. HOLD IT!

TERRY. Our initial marketing strategy –

BOB. STOP STOP STOP!

*(**BOB** yanks apart two extension cords. Silence. Everyone stops and looks at **BOB**. The largest **ASSISTANT** stands frozen with sledgehammer raised, ready to strike the octopus. Long pause.)*

McALLISTER. How about thirty-five dollars?

BOB. Can everyone please evacuate my office now?

(slight pause)

McALLISTER. Well, Terry, why don't you take everyone outside. You can leave the stuff, just, go get some coffee.

(He hands her a hundred dollars.)

McALLISTER. *(cont.)* Here, there's a little place around the corner. Come back when you're finished.

*(**TERRY** leaves with her army in tow. They leave everything behind. **BOB** stares at the dying octopus.)*

OK, Bob. What's on your mind?

*(**BOB** walks over to his desk and sits down. The Banderscott lies on his desk. He watches it.)*

BOB. It kills people.

McALLISTER. Oh sure. It's like one of them tazers, but worse. There's no shock or electricity, either. You just touch that red bit there, like that, that's it, you drop dead!

BOB. I see.

McALLISTER. It's a totally revolutionary method of killing somebody. In fact, during the infomercial, we were thinking of pulling up a member of the audience –

BOB. Mr. McAllister.

McALLISTER. Harcourt.

BOB. Sir. Look. As mind-blowing as this invention is, I really think. You need a different marketing strategy. I mean, you can't. Just. How about this.

McALLISTER. OK, you're the expert. I'm all ears.

BOB. I mean, certainly there are other applications. It's really an amazing device. We could market them as exterminator kits, to use on roaches or household pests. The, all purpose Roach-Zapper, kills on contact. It would have to be slightly modified, that's all.

McALLISTER. It doesn't kill roaches.

BOB. What?

McALLISTER. You said roaches?

BOB. Yes.

McALLISTER. It doesn't kill roaches it kills people.

(pause)

BOB. Yes. But. If it works on people, surely we could use it on roaches?

(He slowly and hopefully looks to **DR. THINN**, *who is still huddled in the corner. The doctor looks up to* **BOB** *and coughs.)*

THINN. Um, well, no. Actually, it doesn't seem to work on other animal or vegetable life. Only people.

(pause)

BOB. It only kills people.

McALLISTER. Yes, sirree, Bob.

(pause)

BOB. Its sole application is the killing of human beings. It can't do one other thing.

McALLISTER. We know it's somewhat limited, as opposed to the other products you market, that's why we're willing to offer so much more, the case, the guarantee, certainly the audience will eat up the spork set. And, hell, Bob, you know I was just baiting you. Eventually we'd offer it for only nineteen ninety-five.

BOB. *(evenly)* Why would anyone buy a device designed specifically to kill someone?

McALLISTER. Well, why wouldn't they? Who wouldn't want one of these? People buy guns every day. Nothing beats a Banderscott for home defense. Easy to use. No mess to clean up afterwards. Or, I don't know, use 'em in child rearing, it's a real incentive to obey, let me tell you.

BOB. Sir. *(beat)* I'm flabbergasted. The fact that such an object has been made. It's like witnessing the birth of the atom bomb.

McALLISTER. It is a great time to be alive, Bob!

BOB. Who created this perversity? *(He rounds on* **THINN**.*)* Is that your part in all this?

McALLISTER. Oh, yes, indeed, Bob, Dr. Thinn is the developer of the Banderscott and owns all patent rights.

BOB. You're a monster. I've seen hundreds of sleazebags, charlatans, quacks, snake-oil salesman, lawyers, agents, and telemarketers in my day, but you, sir, are the lowest specimen of humanity that ever crawled out of the sewers of Texas.

McALLISTER. Oh, he's from New Jersey.

THINN. DON'T YOU THINK I KNOW IT'S TRUE? YOU THINK I CAN'T SEE THE LOGICAL CONCLUSION?

(**THINN** *screams in primal rage and throws himself onto* **BOB***'s desk, scooping up the Banderscott. He bonks himself in the center of the forehead with the red tip. He seems to sustain no injury, but he immediately collapses to the floor, stricken dead.*)

BOB. Oh my God.

McALLISTER. Aw, not again.

BOB. Oh God, Eileen!

McALLISTER. Well, this is just a pain in the ass. That's the sixth time that's happened this week.

BOB. EILEEN!

McALLISTER. Well, at least you can see the product in action. You see how immediate the effect is, check his pulse, that man's dead.

BOB. SHIT EILEEN WHERE ARE YOU?

EILEEN. (*from off*) Sir?

BOB. Call an ambulance!

McALLISTER. Call an ambulance? Hey, now, Bob, there's no need for that.

BOB. The man is dead!

McALLISTER. Sure he's dead, that what it does, he'll be fine in a few minutes.

BOB. This.

(**BOB** *freezes. Very slowly, his head rotates up to* **McALLISTER**. *Long silence.*)

What.

McALLISTER. He'll be fine, it only lasts a little while. After it wears off, he'll be up and walking around again. Didn't I mention that?

(pause)

BOB. How. Is that. Possible?

McALLISTER. Ain't it amazing? For only nineteen ninety-five, Bob!

BOB. This device. Kills you. And then you come back from the dead?

McALLISTER. Absolutely. It just wears off after a while. *(Suddenly, for once,* **McALLISTER** *becomes irritated.)* Now hang on here, Bob. You thought I was selling you a device that killed people for good? Well, that's screwed up, Bob. I'm talking up and down and back and forth with a big possum. Why would you use that on your kid, that's infanticide, Bob! Who do you take me for?

BOB. I.

McALLISTER. *(cheerful again)* Aw, you know what, forget it, Bob, an honest mistake. But, yes, there it is, the Banderscott, kills people dead, how's that for a slogan, and the best part is, you kill 'em, and in a little while, they're all right and ready to go again!

(Long pause. **BOB** *picks up the Banderscott and holds it to the light.)*

BOB. That is. *(awed silence)* There exists no adjective to describe what I'm feeling about this product.

McALLISTER. And it's guaranteed!

BOB. I'm giddy. I'm terrified. I feel as if God has reached into me. What I hold in my hand, the human race has sought since it crawled out of the primordial sludge. *(pause)* That would make a great intro.

McALLISTER. Do we have a deal, Bob?

BOB. Are you kidding? You hand me the universe in a light-weight, space-age pen case and ask me if I'm in? I'm in!

McALLISTER. Welcome to the team, Bob.

BOB. Jesus Christ. *(He indicates* **THINN**.*)* Is he really going to wake up?

McALLISTER. Should be a few more minutes.

BOB. What does he say it's like?

McALLISTER. Um. Peaceful. *(He smiles.)* Actually, he said it was boring. I don't think that's very good PR, though. Still, nothing we can do about that. We didn't invent the afterlife, we just get you there.

BOB. Boring, huh? Jeez, that's a shame. You said this happened before? Other people using it like this?

McALLISTER. Oh, no, just him.

BOB. Just him? He killed himself six times?

McALLISTER. This week he killed himself six times. Lord knows I've lost count over the last few months.

BOB. Why?

McALLISTER. Well. *(He looks at* **THINN**, *then, confidentially:)* Is this off the books, Bob?

BOB. Oh, yeah, sure.

McALLISTER. Well, the first time Dr. Thinn used it, he used it on himself. He has his problems, the doctor, in fact, we think that's why he developed it in the first place, to, you know, do himself in. He's just not good with violent death, didn't want to hang himself, drown himself, you know. Well, one day, we just found him with this thing on the floor of his office. We had no idea it was reversible, not then.

BOB. Sure.

McALLISTER. Well, about twenty-two hours later he wakes up, that's how long it takes the first time, twenty-two hours. And he's fine, and that's when we really knew we were onto something. Well, the good doctor's a little frazzled, so he takes the thing and kills himself again. Now, this time, he comes back a little sooner, maybe twenty hours. See that's the problem we're still working out, the people who use it seem to develop a, uh, whatdoyoucallit, like with alcohol.

BOB. A tolerance?

McALLISTER. That's it, a tolerance. That's what the Doctor called it. So, we let it go on. Sometimes the poor man just has to go off and kill himself. Each time he comes back a little sooner, so he gets back to work a little quicker! Ha!

BOB. Wow. If he's really that suicidal, you might want to get him help.

McALLISTER. We tried, believe me. But he just won't hear it. These days I can hardly get to see him while he's alive anymore.

BOB. That's too bad. Wait. If he knows he's just going to come back, why does he keep using the Banderscott? I'm fairly certain there are other ways to kill yourself.

McALLISTER. Oh, he gave in and tried. One day, we found him in his office, hanging from the ceiling fan. They cut him down but it was too late, dead on arrival to the hospital. Still, twenty minutes after he was pronounced dead, there he was again, walking out on his own two feet. Next day we found him with sleeping pills. Took fifty of 'em. Dead again, but that time we didn't even bother with the hospital. He got up and went back to work half an hour later.

BOB. Wait. So. He won't die?

McALLISTER. Nope. Can't seem to manage it. I think he keeps using the Banderscott in the off-handed chance the thing'll work for good one of these days.

BOB. So he didn't just develop a tolerance to the Banderscott.

McALLISTER. Oh, no, no. He developed a tolerance to *death*.

(*Pause.* **THINN** *suddenly sits straight up.*)

BOB. Oh wow. Oh, Dr. Thinn, I hope you'll accept my deepest apologies. What I said was totally out of line.

THINN. (*grimly*) What did he say to you?

McALLISTER. Now, come on, Doctor, let's put this nonsense behind us.

BOB. I didn't realize you'd be coming back. That changes everything.

THINN. Yes, sir, it certainly CHANGES EVERYTHING. *(***THINN*** slowly becomes more and more hysterical.)* You're going to sell these knickknacks for irresistible prices with every guarantee imaginable, and people will start killing themselves to see what it's like knowing full well they'll be back. Someone's bound to find out that once you start using it, it becomes increasingly more difficult to die at all. Then what? We've guaranteed the immortality of the entire human race. The effects pass from mother to fetus like any other abused substance. In twenty years? Hah. Overpopulation is just a word. You can't comprehend the potential horror. No more food to eat, then no more land to live on, then no room to walk, room to stand, room to breathe, we'll all be crowded face to face as more and more of us are generated, having sex with fourteen people around us simultaneously, eating into our neighbors, and none of us able to die, even as the bodies pile twenty miles high and push us down to the depths of the ocean, unable to breathe, crushed by the pressure, even as our guts hang out and our organs are chewed by those around us in mindless nourishment, even as we become a single, planet-devouring, pulsating organism, we shall not die.

McALLISTER. Oh, Doctor. You really have a flair for the overdramatic.

THINN. Give me the device.

BOB. No. I don't want you killing yourself again. I need to think about this.

McALLISTER. What is there to think about? The man's a glutton for depression. It's a wonder product, of course there's going to be a few namby pambies talking gloom and doom.

THINN. Give it to me, dammit!

(**THINN** *leaps at* **BOB** *and grabs hold of the Banderscott. He and* **BOB** *fight over it, each trying to retain his grip, and* **BOB** *trying desperately to avoid the deadly red bulb.*)

BOB. No. Let go!

McALLISTER. Bob, Dr. Thinn, please. This is infantile.

THINN. LET GO!

BOB. Doctor, come on! Let go!

McALLISTER. Doctor, you have to see the bright side of this. You have to see this from a sales perspective. Gentlemen, please. Can't we just –

(**THINN** *lets go.* **BOB** *smacks* **McALLISTER** *in the head. The Texan collapses, dead. At that exact moment,* **TERRY** *and her troops have entered the doorway, looking to see what the trouble is.*)

BOB. Oh, crap.

TERRY. You killed Mr. McAllister!

BOB & THINN. Harcourt.

TERRY. You killed Harcourt! Get him!

BOB. Wait –

(*Too late.* **TERRY** *flies at him, grabbing for the Banderscott, followed by the* **ASSISTANTS** *who grab the sledgehammer, the octopus, and every weapon available. A fray ensues.* **BOB**, *attempting to defend himself, kills every other person in the room with the Banderscott, shrieking out violently. He finally stops screaming and surveys the bodies, lunatic with battle lust.*)

BOB. I AM GOD NOW. I CONTROL LIFE AND DEATH AND ALL THE INFOMERCIALS. THE FUTURE OF THE HUMAN RACE LIES IN MY HAND. WHO DARES OPPOSE ME?

(*A tweed-jacketed man opens the door cautiously, humbly.* **BOB** *stares at him.*)

BOB. Warren Edds?

WARREN. Hi, Bob. Is this a bad time?

BOB. Somewhat. I think I'm in a state of clinical shock. I've just killed several people. One of them twice. But I just remembered that they weren't the ones I wanted to kill, Warren.

WARREN. Oh?

BOB. Not at all. I wanted to kill you. And now, I think I can actually afford the pleasure.

*(**BOB** lunges, **WARREN** parries. **WARREN** notices **McALLISTER** among the dead.)*

WARREN. That's Harcourt McAllister, isn't it? You've got his little death-thingy that he's peddling around.

BOB. C'mere, Mr. Tabloid Messiah!

WARREN. Lemme ask you something, Bob, before you send me to meet my maker.

BOB. Ask away, Warren.

WARREN. How much would you pay for that?

BOB. Pay for what?

WARREN. The luxury of killing me.

BOB. What?

WARREN. How about your soul? Would you pay for it with your soul?

*(**BOB** lunges again, missing. He grows progressively more disheartened.)*

BOB. I'm in marketing. I never needed my soul before. Come on, Warren, you're fighting for your life. You'll need to offer me something better than that.

WARREN. OK. How about I throw in your sense of decency and a free apron?

*(Stab and a miss. **WARREN** is in full-out sales mode now.)*

But wait, Bob, because you'll give up even more! For that one moment of guilty pleasure, you'll be well on your way to fully accepting the consequences of selling out the planet earth for a couple of dollars. You'll throw in your self-image, your conscience, and your own mother. Still not enough? How about fifteen bottles of fine scotch whiskey that you'll drink to numb the horror over the next six months? And I'll throw in my personal guarantee that you'll never, ever, one hundred percent ever be able to look yourself in the mirror again. What's that worth to you, Bob? Are you ready to kill one more person at that unbelievable price?

(**BOB** *finally relents. He slumps to his knees.*)

BOB. No.

WARREN. Say again, Bob, I couldn't hear you.

BOB. It's not worth it, Warren. I won't buy that.

WARREN. Then give me that thing.

(**BOB** *hands the Banderscott over to* **WARREN**.)

BOB. Thank you, Warren.

WARREN. Any time, Bob. That's what a good salesman's for. Lets you see what you really want. I'm going to put this in a safe place. I'll have my people call your people.

(**WARREN** *begins to go. He indicates the bodies.*)

Don't have anyone call these people. They're out of control.

(*He leaves.* **BOB** *reflects for a moment.* **THINN** *sits up again. He gets his bearings.*)

THINN. What happened?

BOB. The Banderscott is gone.

THINN. Really?

BOB. Yeah.

THINN. How?

BOB. Warren Edds came and took it away.

THINN. Unbelievable. He was the one who stole my double-sided toothbrush, too.

(**THINN** *picks up the sledgehammer.*)

Not this time, Warren!

(*He runs from the room, leaving* **BOB** *alone among the dead.* **BOB** *slowly gets his coat and heads for the door.*)

BOB. Eileen?

EILEEN. *(from off)* Yes, sir.

BOB. I'm going out for a while. Cancel my calls, and hold my appointments.

EILEEN. How long will you be out, sir?

(**BOB** *eyes the bodies.*)

BOB. About twenty-two hours.

(He shuts the door on the spectacle of mortality.)

End of Play

ABOUT THE AUTHORS
and THE PORCH ROOM

Pete Barry is a playwright, screenwriter, actor, director and musician. His short play, *Drop* (co-written with Michael DeAngelis), was a winner of the 2009 Samuel French Off Off Broadway Short Play Festival. His plays *Nine Point Eight Meters Per Second Per Second* and *The Banderscott* were also official selections. His screenplay *10 Crimes in 2 Hours* was a finalist in the 13th Annual Writers Network Screenplay and Fiction Competition.

He is a cofounder of the Porch Room and has co-produced and co-directed several collections of short plays, including *Five Cornered Thinking* at the New York Comedy Club and *Burt Reynolds' Amazing Napalm Powered Oven and Other Paid Programming* in the 2001 New York Fringe Festival. He shared the 2009 NJACT Perry Award for Outstanding Production of an Original Play for *Accidents Happen*.

Pete lives in the Lehigh Valley in Pennsylvania with his wife Jean and his daughter Lia.

John P. Dowgin is a playwright, screenwriter, director, and actor. He has been involved in theater since the age of 13, and sees no sign of the condition improving anytime soon. His one-act plays *The Fruppum, Alabama Chamber of Commerce* and *Some Colors on a Wall* have both been official selections of the Samuel French Off Off Broadway Short Play Festival, and have since been produced by numerous theaters in New York, Los Angeles, and New Jersey. A number of his screenplays are also in a place called 'development,' which he suspects to be a purely theoretical dimension somewhere between Purgatory and Oz.

John is a cofounder of The Porch Room and has co-produced and/or co-directed productions including *Five Cornered Thinking* at the New York Comedy Club and *Burt Reynolds' Amazing Napalm Powered Oven and Other Paid Programming* in the 2001 New York Fringe Festival. He shared the 2009 NJACT Perry Award for Outstanding Production of an Original Play for *Accidents Happen*.

John lives in New Jersey with his wife Faith and his son Caden.

J. Michael DeAngelis is a writer, actor and director. His short play, *Drop* (co-written with Pete Barry), was a winner of the 2009 Samuel French Off Off Broadway Short Play Festival. He has written or co-written the plays *Reunion Special, Reverie* and *Signs from God*. He starred in and co-wrote the short film *Tails Between Their Legs*, which was a winner of the National Film Challenge. *And God Spoke...*, a comedy pilot he wrote and directed, aired on SETV in Pennsylvania. He shared the 2009 NJACT Perry Award for Outstanding Production of an Original Play for *Accidents Happen*.

He is the Managing Director of the Porch Room, where he has written and performed in *An Evening on the Porch, Accidents Happen* and the short film *Early Morning in the Tenement.*

Michael lives in Philadelphia with his collection of betamax video tapes and his flask of aged scotch.

The Porch Room is an independent theater and film company, whose works have been recognized in the Samuel French Off Off Broadway Short Play Festival, The New York International Fringe Festival, The Philly Fringe Festival, The Triggerstreet.com Film Festival, The Piper Theater's Living Series, *Fade In* Magazine, The Writer's Network and The National Film Challenge. Visit www.porchroom.com for more information.

OTHER TITLES AVAILABLE FROM SAMUEL FRENCH

OFF OFF BROADWAY FESTIVAL PLAYS, 34TH SERIES

Various authors

One of Manhattan's most established play festivals, the Samuel French Off Off Broadway Short Play Festival fosters the work of emerging writers, giving them the exposure of publication and representation.

The festival resulting in this collection was held July 14th-19th, 2009 at The Main Stage Theatre on 42nd Street in New York City.

From the initial pool of over 715 submissions, the Final Forty plays were chosen to be performed over a period of one week. A panel of judges comprised of celebrity playwrights, theatrical agents and artistic directors nominated one or more of each evening's plays as finalists. The final round was then held on the last day of the festival. Out of these plays, six winners listed below were chosen by Samuel French, Inc. to receive publication and licensing contracts.

Winning plays and playwrights for this collection include:

Drop by J. Michael DeAngelis and Pete Barry

The Education Of Macoloco by Jen Silverman

realer than that by Kitt Lavoie

The Student by Matt Hoverman

Thucydides by Scott Elmegreen and Drew Fornarola

Just Knots by Christina Gorman

OTHER TITLES AVAILABLE FROM SAMUEL FRENCH

CHRISTMAS SHORTS

Matt Hoverman

Collection of short plays / Holiday Comedy

A celebrated Winner of the 2009 Samuel French Off Off Broadway Short Play Festival, playwright Matt Hoverman brings an evening of hilarious short holiday comedies to the stage. A wonderful alternative for theatres tired of mounting the traditional seasonal play, Christmas Shorts offers five original plays that humorously comment on holiday themes: family, the nativity, Xmas cards, and elves. An outstanding Christmas collection for any theatre!

Included are the plays: *Going Home, The Christmas Witch, Xmas Cards, Nativity,* and the Samuel French Festival award-winning play *The Student.*

OTHER TITLES AVAILABLE FROM SAMUEL FRENCH

FRESH BREWED

Henry Meyerson

Cast of 2m, 2f

Fresh Brewed is a collection of eleven plays, all of which take place in a coffee bar, all of which use the same set of two small tables and four chairs, and all of which can be performed by two male and two female actors in various combinations from a monologue to two quartets.

"...an incredible 55-minute show that held my interest every minute. These eight short vignettes, with four actors playing various roles, were real "slice of life" and so fascinating, you had the impression that maybe 15 or so actors were taking part...I love good writing as much as I love good songwriting, so it was double my pleasure this time out. This is not quite a 'family show' so parents be advised. But it is a comic evening with a twist - there are truly thoughtful insights interspersed with the clever, humorous dialog.
Truly, not to be missed!
– *Stu Hamsta's Cabaret Hotline*

OTHER TITLES AVAILABLE FROM SAMUEL FRENCH

ALL THE KING'S WOMEN

Luigi Jannuzzi

Full Length, Comedy / 3f, 1m or up to 17f, 7m, or an all Female cast

The story of Elvis Presley told through the eyes of 17 Women! Some Enthralled! Some Appalled, ALL OBSESSED! A fast paced series of 5 comedic plays and 3 monologues based on the Life of Elvis Presley. From Tupelo Mississippi where 11 year old Elvis wanted a BB Gun instead of a guitar, to The Steve Allen Show, from President Richard Nixon's office, to Andy Warhol's studio, from Cadillac Salesmen, to Graceland guards, this is a touching, bring-the-family comedy with a heart that captures the effects that fame, generosity & just being a nice guy can bring to others!

"Perfect Monologues"
– *Outer Critics Circle*

"Jannuzzi has a good ear for the periods and for his characters allowing his actors to show range. The point is perhaps not so much about Elvis per se, but instead these scenes reveal snapshots of an American culture, people, and place."
– *NYTheatre.com*

His plays unfold in such an intimate and genuine way. He writes about Elvis Presley fans with educated and unconventional twists."
– *RobertaontheArts.com*

"Bravo. Much Applause."
– Mario Fratti

"Jannuzzi worked with his biographical and dramatic material with smooth transitions and captivating creativity."
– *RobertaontheArts.com*

"In a nearly chronological order, the stand-alone scenes take place between the 1940s and the present day. Each scene is listed in the program with a date and location, driving home the point that these characters and situations are best understood within the context of their period."
– *NYTheatre.com*

SAMUELFRENCH.COM